BLACK DIAMONDS.

BLACK DIAMONDS

GATHERED IN THE

DARKEY HOMES OF THE SOUTH.

BY

EDWARD A. POLLARD,

OF VIRGINIA.

New-York:

PUDNEY & RUSSELL, PUBLISHERS,

No. 79 John-Street.

1859.

PREFATORY.

THE writer of these simple pages has prepared them for publication from a collection of hasty and unstudied letters, on the subject of slave life in the South, which were originally addressed to DAVID M. CLARKSON, Esq., "Glenbrook," Newburgh, N. Y., a gentleman whose friendship is one among those in the North that he has greatly prized, and whose cultivated patriotism is of that broad and noble type that he has ever fervently admired. The letters are not elaborated: the author wrote them from what he found in his heart. Whether he shall add still further to them will depend upon the reception by the public of this humble offering.

"SLAVE LIFE IN THE SOUTH."*

In general we are strongly averse to mixing up special questions in ethics or in politics with what is called polite literature. Artistically viewed, we doubt whether the mixture is ever allowable. Even satiric poetry, we take it, forms no exception to the rule ; for it is the province of that species of literature to attack wickedness and folly from the standpoint of admitted maxims of morality and wisdom, not to agitate debatable or unsettled problems. The introduction into the novel or poem of subjects pertaining to strict polemics or to severe philosophy, as the main purpose of the work, produces an incongruous association, which is never agreeable and is often disgusting. Who wants to read a novel designed to illustrate the beauties of free trade or a protective tariff? Who *does* read Montgomery's maudlin poem, or Longfellow's sentimental cant in rhyme, on the awful sin of negro slavery? Since the publication of Mrs. Stowe's "Uncle Tom's Cabin," which led the van of a frightful procession of books of a similar order on both sides of the slavery question, every reader of experience, taste, and discrimination, is predisposed to turn with loathing from any issue from the press whose title page has a perceptible squinting toward the vexed and vexatious subject. He is inclined to avoid it as a premeditated bore and deliberate swindle—a delusion and a snare—a cunning "dodge," by which he may be made the victim of self-inflicted twaddle. Of course there is frequently much matter of pith and moment in the numerous books in which the discussion of the slavery question, in all or a few of its aspects, is thrown into the shape of stories or sketches. Indeed, there are some that touch the subject in a way so incidental and natural, and with so little of a partisan or disputatious spirit, that if the predisposition against them be once overcome, they may be read with equal entertainment and instruction.

* From the *New Orleans Delta*, Editorial.

Among the last productions to which we allude, we unhesitatingly place a small and unpretending volume, being a series of short sketches of slave life in the South, in the form of letters originally addressed by the author, Edward A. Pollard, of Washington City, to his friend, David M. Clarkson, of Newburgh, New York.

The author appears to be a thorough Southerner in education, opinion, sympathy, and attachment; yet, his letters are *remarkably free from sectional prejudice and acerbity*, and, in truth, contain sketches that are amongst the *most catholic, and tolerant, and genial*, we ever had occasion to peruse. He would seem to have travelled much, to have observed much, and to know much of various countries and peoples. But the negro nature he especially knows, profoundly, intimately; knows it, not by intellection merely, but also by heart; knows it, not through the cold light of ethnological science only, but most of all, through the warm, enkindling recollections of boyhood and youth. The negro, who, in his true nature, is always a boy, let him be ever so old, is better understood by a boy, than by a whole academy of philosophers, unless the boy element in the said philosophers is unusually long-lived and prosperous. The author, in this case, guided by his boy-knowledge of the negro, cannot misconceive or untruthfully delineate him. How appreciative, how loving, how tender and sympathetic, he is in his delineations, we will let a few extracts show.

*　　*　　*　　*　　*

LETTER OF THANKS FROM THE AUTHOR TO HORACE GREELEY, ESQ.

WASHINGTON, JUNE 20, 1859.

HORACE GREELEY, ESQ.,
Editor New-York Tribune.

MY DEAR SIR: I undoubtedly owe you many thanks for the extraordinary and flattering marks of attention you have bestowed upon my little book of sketches of Slave Life in the South. You have not made them the subject of an ordinary "book notice." You have not bestowed upon them an obscure and stinted paragraph in the literary corner of the *Tribune.* But you have done me the honor of devoting a long editorial to the special subject of the interest of my literary performance. That I have not acknowledged this extraordinary honor sooner has not been, I assure you, my dear sir, for lack of appreciation, but in waiting for occasion to mature wherein I might make my acknowledgments most properly to you.

I was aware that the subject of my little book (the "almighty nigger") was a tender one with you. I had, I must confess, also heard among the miserable, ignorant people of the South many bad accounts of you. You had been represented to me as a curious old man, doting on "niggers," and deriding all white persons who fancied themselves superior to your idols. Indeed, report said, that you had taken your models for manners from the negroes, and that, in speaking of your superiors, you were in the habit of adopting that coarse insolence sometimes displayed by Cuffy in adverting to white people at a distance.

Can you then be surprised, sir, that, with such slanders of you made familiar to my mind, I should have heard with some degree of tremulousness that you had devoted a long editorial of criticism to my unobtrusive little book. I naturally concluded from the slanders current in relation to you that your criticism was very adverse; first, because it was my misfortune to be born in the South, and secondly, because I had propitiated neither political party by that coarse abuse which has heretofore been made the appanage of all the controvertists on the subject of slavery. I had indeed sought to shun in my book anything that was sectional in an odious sense. I had conceived the idea of regarding the negro as one of the most fruitful and innocent topics of our literature, rather than as a firebrand of partisan controversy. Enough, however, was to be gathered from my pages to show that I did not sympathize with your own peculiar creed of nigger-idolatry. I therefore feared that the subject of my little book had been tortured by you into a sectional discussion, and that you had, rather as the politician than as the man, visited your censure upon my humble and defenceless head.

Judge my surprise—my great relief—my gratification, in fact, to find that, so far from treating my book with sectional acerbity, you had overlooked the vexed question in its literary features, had commended its innocent beauties of sentiment, and had mentioned side by side with some of the touching tales of the classics, the little domestic stories it contains. You compliment its heartfulness; you speak of the indulgence of the author in "the pleasures of memory," and say "the way in which he does it is creditable to his heart." I thank you, sir, for this; for sincerity and tenderness I esteem no light virtues of style. But, sir, I am surprised to find you remark that you have not received a copy of the book. You appear to have praised it from detached passages you have seen in the press. One extract you particularly distinguish in your praise, and you say of this:

"It has been disintegrated, if we may say so, from the main work, and, in the highly respectable character of an Elegant Extract, is now making a fashionable tour through the newspapers. We trust that the Reverend Doctor Adams has seen this wandering small paragraph; that it has rendered moist his venerable eyes, and warmed the cockles of his ancient heart."

Sir, I can only say, in the fulness of my heart, that I shall immediately supply you with several newly-printed copies of my book which you will observe I have done you the compliment of entitling "Black Diamonds," from a term which you have applied in your own criticism of it. And I trust, sir, that not only the "wandering small paragraph," but others of similar pathos may warm the cockles of your own heart, as well as that of Dr. Adams.

The main object with which I wrote the pages you commend was to present some natural portraits of negro character. The tenor of your criticism shows to what degree you esteem me to have attained in that respect. And your judgment in this matter, my dear sir, I recognize as of extraordinary value, on account of your relations to the negro. You know the negro, not as myself from the distant observation of the master, but from the contact of companionship. You know him from mingling with him, and from brotherhood with him. Your criticism, therefore, I gladly and proudly accept as a judgment of the naturalness of my descriptions.

In one respect of your article, you must allow me, my dear sir, to correct you in point of information. I am not, as you conjecture, an "impoverished office-holder." Appearances, too, are only against me when you judge, that, of all the population of the federal metropolis, myself seems to be in the lowest spirits, "if we except Mr. James Buchanan." I am, thank you, sir, in tolerable spirits; am not a member of the kitchen-cabinet; am a plain man, without office of trust or profit; and am fond of niggers in my peculiar way, but without embracing in my affection for them free love, free wool, and "the forty thieves."

In conclusion, I hope, my dear sir, that you will remember the good words I have addressed you, should I again fall into your hands. When my Southern friends have warned me of your ire, I have invariably responded with good words of you. In this, I have taken a lesson from that sapient old negro, Uncle Junk, of whose wisdom I have given some brief account in my book. At one time, a minister was telling Uncle

Junk, to work him to repentance, how the devil tormented those who went to hell. Junk hoped that "good Mass'r Debble" wouldn't be so cruel. The minister reproved him for speaking of Satan in such polite terms. "Well, you see, Mass'r," replied the old negro, "no tellin' but de enemy might cotch me, and den I trust he remember as how I spoked of him perlitely, and jes de same as if he was a white man."

I remain, Sir,

Your obliged, humble servant,

EDWD. A. POLLARD.

CONTENTS.

LETTER I.

LETTER II.

LETTER III.

LETTER IV.

LETTER V.

LETTER VI.

LETTER VII.

LETTER VIII.

LETTER IX.

LETTER X.

LETTER XI.

BLACK DIAMONDS.

LETTER I.

MACON, GEORGIA, 1858.

MY DEAR C——: I engaged to write you from the South, and I take the earliest opportunity to date my correspondence from Middle Georgia. But I should not fail to drop you a line or two, at start, of Macon, where I write, as it is accounted one of the most beautiful cities of the South, and has many objects of interest. It is the seat of several public institutions, but has very little trade. Near by the city, on a commanding position, stands Fort Hawkins, a rude wooden building, which was constructed as a protection against the Indians; for you must know that Macon was about the frontier of Georgia in 1818. An Indian mound is in sight, on the top of which are standing a few tall, melancholy pines. On the hills which surround the city, and in the beautiful little vill of Vineville, which adjoins it, may be seen the evidences of refinement, in the handsome residences adorned with shrubbery and evergreens; among which the olive and the holly, with its lucid green, are the most common. Many of the residences of men of wealth are admirable, especially for their tasteful grounds. But there is the fondness for white paint, which may be observed in all parts of the South, and for a nondescript architecture, in which all styles are jumbled; or a plain magnificence studied in rows of pillars and flights of steps, which frequently give to a Southern villa the singular appearance of an eleemosynary institution. The chief object, however, to which the admiration of the stranger is directed in Macon is the public cemetery, which is compared (not extravagantly) in some points of natural scenery, to Mount Auburn and Greenwood. It is a lovely piece of ground, with natural terraces overhanging the Ocmulgee, and the wild glen that divides it. The picturesque effect, however, is almost entirely destroyed by the thick brushwood, which prevents the eye from taking in the outlines of the scene. The ground is covered with coppices of oak and pine, and studiously kept in a state of nature. It seems, however, a strange idea to keep the natural scene concealed by the brushwood which everywhere intercepts the view. Maybe, it is intended to be

"Unadorned, adorned the most"—

an æsthetic fogyism, *en passant*, disproved and despised, at least by the charming ladies of Macon.

In writing to you, my dear C., of the South and its *peculiar institution* (as I intend), I am sure that I have no prejudice to dispel from your mind on the subject; but as I may hereafter publish some extracts from the correspondence, I hope the sketches, which may amuse you, may correct the false views of others, derived, as they chiefly are, from the libels of Northern spies, who live or travel here in disguise. Thus I observed lately a communication in some of the Abolition papers, professing to have been written by one who has been a resident of Macon for eleven years, to the effect that the people here do not allow Northern papers to circulate or be taken by subscribers, or even Congressional documents to be among them, which do not harmonize with their peculiar views. Although this infamous libel is quite as absurd and undeserving of contradiction as the famed Arrowsmith hoax, or any of the Sanguinary Crowbar style of negro-worship fictions, it deserves notice in one respect. There are a number of Yankee doughfaces in the South, who, before us, are the greatest admirers of the *peculiar institution*, and, to honey-fuggle us, even chime in with the abuse of their own section. There is danger in these men of disguised character, many of whom are doing business in the South. They are not to be trusted; and while, not satisfied with being tolerated among us, they impose on our confidence and hospitality by their professions, they take secret opportunities to gratify their real hatred of us, by tampering with the slaves, or by libelling the South under the shelter of anonymous letters published in the North. The man who would devise a safe opportunity to publish what he knew to be false and libellous of those whose good will he had won by another lie, might, with the same hope of impunity, venture on a grander revenge, and secretly conspire with the slave in a rebellion.

But it is not my purpose to trouble you with a dissertation on "the vexed question," or the social system of the South, or any of the political aspects of Slavery. I merely design to employ a few leisure hours in a series of unpretending sketches of the condition, habits, and peculiarities of the negro-slave. The field, you know, has furnished a number of books; and I am sure, my dear C., that you are too sensible of the large share of public attention *niggers* occupy in this country to slight them. Besides, I am thoroughly convinced that the negro portraits of the fiction writers are, most of them, mere caricatures, taking them all, from "Uncle Tom's Cabin," down to the latest reply thereto—"a book" from a Virginia authoress, in which the language put in the mouth of her leading character is a mixture of Irish idioms with the dialect of the Bowery. Who ever heard a Southern negro say, as the Virginia lady's sable hero does, "The tip-top of the morning to you, young ladies!" or "What's to pay now?" Nor will we find any of

Mrs. Stowe's *Uncle Toms* in the South, at least so far as the religious portraiture goes. The negro, in his religion, is not a solemn old gentleman, reading his Bible in corners and praying in his closet: his piety is one of fits and starts, and lives on prayer-meetings, with its rounds of *'zortations*, shoutings, and stolen sweets of baked pig.

You already know my opinion of the peculiarities of the negro's condition in the South, in the provision made for his comfort, and in the attachment between him and his master. The fact is, that, in wandering from my native soil to other parts of the world, I have seen slavery in many forms and aspects. We have all heard enough of the colliers and factory operatives of England, and the thirty thousand costermongers starving in the streets of London; as also of the serfs and crown-peasants of Russia, who are considered not even as chattels, but as part of the land, and who have their wives selected for them by their masters. I have seen the hideous slavery of Asia. I have seen the coolies of China "housed on the wild sea with wilder usages," or creeping with dejected faces into the suicide houses of Canton. I have seen the Siamese slave creeping in the presence of his master on all-fours—a human quadruped. It was indeed refreshing, after such sights, to get back to the Southern institution, which strikes one after so many years of absence, with a novelty that makes him appreciate more than ever the evidences of comfort and happiness on the plantations of the South.

The first unadulterated negro I had seen for a number of years (having been absent for the most of that time on a foreign soil), was on the railroad cars in Virginia. He looked like *home*. I could have embraced the old uncle, but was afraid the passengers, from such a demonstration, might mistake me for an abolitionist. I looked at him with my face aglow, and my eyelids touched with tears. How he reminded me of my home—of days gone by—that poetry of youth, "when I was a boy," and wandered with my sable playmates over the warm, wide hills of my sweet home, and along the branches, fishing in the shallow waters with a crooked pin! But no romancing with the past! So we continue our journey onward to "the State of railways and revolvers."

Arrived in Georgia, I find plenty of the real genuine *woolly-heads*, such as don't part their hair in the middle, like Mass'r Fremont. My first acquaintance is with Aunt Debby. I insist upon giving her a shake of the hand, which she prepares for by deprecatingly wiping her hand on her apron. Aunt Debby is an aged colored female of the very highest respectability, and, with her white apron, and her head mysteriously enveloped in the brightest of bandannas, she looks (to use one of her own rather obscure similes) "like a new pin." She is very fond of usurping the authority of her mistress below stairs, and has the habit of designating every one of her own color, not admitted to equality, as "*de nigger*." Aunt Debby is rather spoiled, if having things her own way means it. If at times her mistress is roused to dispute her authority, Aunt Debby is sure to resume the reins when quiet ensues. "Debby," cries her mistress, "what's all this noise in the kitchen—what are you whipping Lucy for?" "La, missis, I'se jest makin' her 'have herself. She too busy *walling* her eyes at me, and spilt the water on the steps." Among the children, Aunt Debby is a great character. She is, however, very partial; and her favorite is little Nina, whom she calls (from what remote analogy we are at a loss to conjecture) "her *jelly-pot*." I flatter myself that I am in her good graces. Her attention to me has been shown by a present of ground-peas, and accessions of fat lightwood to my fire in the morning.

The religious element is very strong in Aunt Debby's character, and her *repertoire* of pious minstrelsy is quite extensive. Her favorite hymn is in the following words, which are repeated over and over again:

"Oh run, brother, run! Judgment day is comin'!
Oh run, brother, run! Why don't you come along?
The road so rugged, and the hill so high—
And my Lord call me home,
To walk the golden streets of my New Jerusalem."

Aunt Debby's religion is of that sort—always begging the Lord to take her up to glory, and professing the greatest anxiety to go *right now!* This religious enthusiasm, however, is not to be taken at its word.

You have doubtless heard the anecdote of Cæsar, which is too good not to have been told more than once; though even if you have heard the story before, it will bear repetition for its moral. Now, Cæsar one day had caught it, not from Brutus, but from Betty—an allegorical coquette in the shape of a red cowhide. On retiring to the silence of his cabin at night, Cæsar commenced to soliloquize, rubbing the part of his body where the castigation had been chiefly administered, and bewailing his fate with tragic desperation, in the third person. "Cæsar," said he, "most done gone—don't want to live no longer! Jist come, good Lord, swing low de chariot, and take dis chile away! Cæsar ready to go—he *wants* to go!" An irreverent darkey outside, hearing these protestations, tapped at the door. "Who dar?" replied Cæsar, in a low voice of suppressed alarm. "De angel of de Lord come for Cæsar, 'cordin to request." The dread summons had indeed come, thought Cæsar; but blowing out the light with a sudden whiff, he replied, in an unconcerned tone, "*De nigger don't live here.*"

There is one other trait wanting to complete Aunt Debby's character. Though at an advanced age, she is very coquettish; and keeps up a regular assault on a big lout of the name of Sam, whom she affects to despise as "jist de meanest nigger de Lord ever put breath in." I overheard some words between them last holidoy. "I'se a white man to-day," says Sam, "and I'se not gwine to take any of your imperence, old ooman;" at the same time, taking the familiar liberty of poking his finger into her side like a brad-awl. "Get 'long, Sa—ten!" replied Aunt Debby, with a shove, but a smile at the same time, to his infernal majesty. And then they both fell to laughing for the space of half a minute, although I must confess, that I could not understand what they were laughing at.

Aunt Debby may serve you, my dear C., as a picture of the happy, contented, Southern slave. Some of your Northern politicians would represent the slaves of the South as sullen, gloomy, isolated from life—in fact, pictures of a living death. Believe me, nothing could be further from the truth. Like Aunt Debby, they have their little prides and passions, their amusements, their pleasantries, which constitute the same sum of happiness as in the lives of their masters.

The whipping-post and the slave mart are constantly paraded before the eyes of the poor, deluded fanatics of your section. Now I can assure you that the inhuman horrors of the slave auction-block exist only in imagination. Many instances of humanity may be observed there; and but seldom does the influence of the almighty dollar appear to sway other and better considerations in the breast of the slaveholder. The separation of families at the block has come to be of very unfrequent occurrence, although the temptation is obvious to do so, as they generally sell much better when the families are separated, and especially as the traders, who usually purchase for immediate realization, do not wish small children. Indeed, there is a statute in this State (Georgia) forbidding the sale of slave children of tender age away from their parents.

I attended a slave auction here the other day. The negroes were called up in succession on the steps of the court-house, where the crier stood. Naturally most of them appeared anxious as the bidding was going on, turning their eyes from one bidder to the other; while the scene would be occasionally enlivened by some jest in depreciation of the negro on the stand, which would be received with especial merriment by his fellow negroes, who awaited their turn, and looked on from a large wagon in which they were placed. As I came up, a second-rate plantation hand of the name of Noah, but whom the crier persisted in calling "Noey," was being offered, it being an administrator's sale. Noey, on mounting the steps, had assumed a most drooping aspect, hanging his head and affecting the feebleness of old age. He had probably hoped to have avoided a sale by a dodge, which is very common in such cases. But the first bid—$1,000—startled him, and he looked eagerly to the quarter whence it proceeded. "Never mind who he is, he has got the money. Now, gentlemen, just go on; who will say fifty?" And so the crier proceeds with his monotonous calling. "I aint worth all that, mass'r; I aint much 'count no how," cries Noey energetically to the first bidder. "Yes, you are, Noey—ah, $1,010, thank you, sir," replies the crier. The gentleman who makes this bid is recognized by Noey as "Mass'r John," one of the heirs. $1,011, rejoins the first bidder, and Noey throws a glance of infinite disdain at him for his presumption in bidding against his master. But as the bidders call over each other, Noey becomes more excited. "Drive on, Mass'r, John," he exclaims, laughing with excitement. The bidding is very slow. Mass'r John evidently hesitates at the last call, $1,085, as too large a price for the slave, though anxious to bid the poor fellow in; but Noey is shouting to him, amid the incitements of the crowd, to "Drive on;" and, after a pause, he says in a firm tone, *eleven hundred dollars.* The crier calls out the round numbers with a decided emphasis. He looks at the first bidder, who is evidently making up his mind whether to go higher, while Noey is regarding him, too, with a look of the keenest suspense. The man shakes his head at last, the hammer falls, and Noey, with an exulting whoop, dashes down the steps to his master.

Yours truly, E. A. P.

To D. M. C., Esq., N. Y.

LETTER II.

MACON, GEORGIA, 1858.

MY DEAR C——: The conclusion of my last letter was, I believe, concerning that abolition bugbear, the slave auction mart. Macon, you must know, is one of the principal marts for slaves in the South. Some time ago, I attended on the city's confines an extraordinarily large auction of slaves, including a gang of sixty-one from a plantation in southwestern Georgia. The prices brought were comparatively low, as there was no warranty of soundness, and owing very much, also, to the fact that the slaves were all sold in families; and they, too, uncommonly large, as I counted fifty-nine negroes in ten families. To give you some idea of the prices brought, I quote the following: Clarinda's family—Clarinda, plantation cook, weakly, 45 years; Betsey, field hand, prime, 22 years; James, field hand, prime, 14 years; Edmond, Betsey's son, 4 years, brought total, $2,620. Jourdon's family, bright mulattoes—Jourdon, blacksmith, prime 33 years; Lindy, field hand, prime, 30 years; Mary, prime, 13 years; Winney, prime, 12 years; Abbey, prime, 9 years; Elizabeth, prime, 6 years, brought total, $3,650. Chloe's family, consisting all of likely negroes, the younger mulattoes—viz.: Chloe, field hand, prime, 33 years, classified as "the best of negroes;" Clarissa, fieldhand, prime, 16 years; Junius, prime, 9 years; Francis, prime, 12 years; Robert, prime, 5 years; infant, 2 months, brought total, $2,940.

During the sale referred to, a lot was put up consisting of a woman and her two sons, one of whom was epileptic (classified by the crier as "fittified"). It was stated that the owner would not sell them unless the epileptic boy was taken along at the nominal price of one dollar, as he wished him provided for. Some of the bidders expressed their dissatisfaction at this, and a trader offered to give two hundred dollars more on condition that the epileptic boy should be thrown out. But the temptation was unheeded, and the poor boy was sold with his mother. There are frequent instances at the auction-block of such humanity as this on the part of masters.

Facts like these should teach us, my dear C., that when that feature even, which we all confess to be the worst in our system of negro-slavery, is relieved by so many instances of humane and generous consideration on the part of slaveholders, our peculiar institution is one the virtues of which qualify its defects, and of peculiar merit.

But I will leave off sermonizing, and give you what I promised—a simple, home picture of slavery.

I must tell you, next to Aunt Debby (who figured in my last letter,) of "Uncle" George—"Old Bones," as we boys used to call him. In our young days we were perpetually either teasing or trading with the old fellow, who was the head-gardener, and was kept constantly on the lookout by our depredations on his vines. Or when we got a few cents from "grandpa," or obtained leave to give away our "old clothes," how we used to buy from him, surreptitiously, little noggins of muddy cider! Years ago, when I left home, he was then almost decrepit from old age, but his avarice and keenness at a trade with his "young mass'rs" were the same as ever. He was a queer-looking old fellow; never would wear a hat; and, with his immense shock of hair as white as snow, and standing off from his head, and his enormous leather "galluses" (suspenders), he made a singular picture in our boyish recollections.

Ah! how many times in years of exile from my native land have I recalled the image of this old slave, with the picture of the old brick garden, with its grass walks and its cherry-trees, and the gentle mounds in the corner, that saddest, sweetest spot on earth—the parental graves!

Boys are never very thoughtful. Nothwithstanding Uncle George's respectability and good nature, we used to worry him very much, and were constantly on the alert to cheat him in a trade. The latter, however, it was difficult to accomplish. Quicksilvered cents, which we used to cunningly offer him, protesting that we had just "found" them, would not go with him. I remember well, when we went out hunting—four brothers, with an old flint gun—how, after shooting a few "peckerwoods" in the orchard, we would go down to the garden and banter Uncle George to shoot at a mark for "fourpence apenny." He was very proud of doing this, and enjoyed the privilege of "shooting a gun" with the same zest as a ten-year-old school boy. But he discovered our trick at last—how the gun was loaded for him without shot and with five "fingers" of powder, "kicking" him most unmercifully, and never showing the least sign on the target.

If you should ever visit "Oakridge," my dear C., you must be prepared for a grand reception by Uncle George, who is quite a Beau Hickman in his way. He is a very genteel beggar. He makes it a point to see all the visitors who come to our home; and has the ugly habit of secretly waylaying them, and begging them to "remember" him. You must have half-a-dollar for him when you come. I think I can promise that you will not be quite as heartless to his appeal for a place in your memory, as was a gentleman from the North ("a friend of humanity"), who lately partook of our hospitality. On his leaving, Uncle George, as usual, exercised his privilege of bringing the horse to "the rack;" and, after assisting the gentleman to mount, begged that "mass'r would *remember* the old nigger." "Oh, yes," replied the friend of humanity, as he rode off, "I will not forget you, my good fellow; I will think of you, and hope you will be elevated into a better condition." But he never gave him a dime to be elevated with.

On the morning following my return home, after years of absence, I was told that Uncle George, who was too decrepit from age to come up to the house, wanted me to come to the negro "quarter" to see him. He understood that I had been in "that gold country," (he meant California) and he wanted to see his young mass'r very particularly, intimating quite clearly that he expected a handsome present. I found the old fellow very comfortably situated. He had grown old gently; he had never seen any hard service; and now in his old age was he not only not required to do any work, but, with that regard commonly exhibited toward the slave when stricken with age, he had every attention paid him in the evening of his life. His meals were sent out to him from our own table. There was one little considerate attention that touched me. His passion for gardening, which had been the whole occupation of his life, had been gratified by giving him a little patch of ground in front of his cabin, where he might amuse himself at his own option.

I found Uncle George in his miniature garden. The old fellow staggered up to see me, and, suddenly dropping, clasped me around the knees. I was quite overcome. This poor old man was "a slave," and yet he had a place in my heart, and I was not ashamed to meet him with tears in my eyes. Miserable abolitionists! you prate of brotherly love and humanity. If you or any man had dared to hurt a hair of this slave, I could have trampled you into the dust.

"Uncle George," said I, "I am sorry to see you look so old." "Ah, mass'r, I'se monstrous old. But missis mighty good to me. She know I set store by all her children. Belinda" (his wife) "*nussed*" (he means 'nursed') "all of you." "Well, Uncle George," I said, "I am glad to see you made so comfortable. The family should never forget you. I have often heard how you saved grandpa's life, when he was drowning." "Yes, yes, mass'r," replied the old fellow, "and I saved him many a dollar, too."

Aunt Belinda, Uncle George's wife, I find in the cabin, as blithe as ever, though stricken with age. She is also on the retired list, and her only care is to "mind" the children in the quarter. The religious element is quite as marked in her character as in that of Aunt Debby, of whom I spoke in my last epistle. But it is more tender and of more universal love. She parts from every one with the wish of "meeting them at the right hand of God." She sings some simple and touching hymns, which I am sorry I did not commit to paper. One she sings very sweetly, in which the lines constantly recur—

Oh, Heaven, sweet Heaven, when shall I see?
When shall I ever get there?

Of another favorite hym of hers I took down the following words:

"Go back, angels! Go back, angels!
Go back into Heaven, little children!
Go back, little angels!
And I don't want to stay behind—
Behold the Lamb of God!
Behold the Lamb of God!
And I don't want to stay behind."

You will find, my dear C., one of the most striking characteristics of the negro in the South in the religious bent of his mind. Whether a member of the church or no, he is essentially at war with the devil. With him religion is entirely a matter of sentiment, and his imagination often takes unwarrantable liberties with the Scriptures. This is particularly so in the images he conjures up of the place where the bad niggers go, and the things appertaining thereto. The negro who has "got de 'ligion," and has never been favored in the process with a peep at "Ole Sa-ten," or is unable to give a full description of his person, is considered by his brethren a doubtful case—a mere trifler, if not a hypocrite.

Sam was relating to me the other day his religious experience, in the course of which, the "Old Scratch" seems to have given him a great deal of trouble, appearing at his elbow whenever he prayed, and walking unceremoniously into his room, cracking a long whip, of which instrument of persuasion Sam seems to have a peculiar horror. "De last time he come," says Sam, "he knock at de door and call 'Sam;' my courage sorter fail me den, and I blows out de light and tell him de nigger done dead two weeks 'go; and den he says, 'If you don't open de door, you dam nigger, I will *straighten* you out;' and den I jis go right clean out of der winder; and as I turn de corner, here come ole mass'r right agin me; and when I tell him as how I jis seed de debble wid my own eyes, he tell me I gwine to catch him, too, and dat he was gwine to get 'ligion out me by *hooping*"—a new use you might imagine, my dear C., to put "hoops" to; but I discovered that Sam's pronunciation was bad, and that he meant nothing more than a dressing to his hide.

But the idea we get of the negro's religion is not always ludicrous. Some of their superstitions are really beautiful, and illustrate their poetic cast of mind. Their hymns, or religious chants, might furnish a curious book. The words are generally very few, and repeated over and over again; and the lines, though very unequal, are sung with a natural cadence that impresses the ear quite agreeably. Most of them relate to the moment of death, and in some of them are simple and poetic images which are often touching. The following occur to me without any pains at selection:

"Oh, carry me away, carry me away, my Lord!
Carry me to the berryin' ground,
The green trees a-bowing. Sinner, fare you well!
I thank the Lord I want to go,
To leave them all behind.
Oh, carry me away, carry me away, my Lord!
Carry me to the berryin' ground."

The following is an image of touching simplicity—a thought of poetry:

"I am gwine home, children; I am gwine home, children,
De angel bid me to come.
I am gwine down to de water side—
Tis de harvest time, children,
And de angel bid me come."

The negroes here have three or four churches of different denominations—Baptist, Methodist, and Presbyterian—in which there is regular service every Sunday. The sermons and exhortations of the colored preachers, as we see them reported, are mostly mere caricatures. They are often sensible, and though the images are those of an untutored imagination, they are anything in the world but ludicrous. I attended the services of one of the negro churches last Sunday, and heard really a very sensible exhortation from one of their colored preachers, who, although he commenced by telling his congregation that "death was knocking at their *heels*," went on to draw a picture of the judgment with a wild, native sublimity that astonished me.

A feature in the services struck me rather ludicrously. The congregation sang a duet, which ran somewhat as follows:

First Voices. Oh, hallelujah! Glory in my soul!

Second Voices. Humph! Whar?

F. V. When the moon go down the mountain, hide your face from God.

S. V. Humph! Whar?

F. V. To talk with Jesus. Glory hallelujah!

The colored Methodist church here is a handsome building, which the negroes have paid for, themselves, besides maintaining a white preacher. You must know that our colored gentry (many of whom, as the custom is here, make considerable money by "hiring their own time," and paying their masters a stated sum for the privilege), not only maintain parsons and build churches, but hire carriages on Sundays to attend them. The fact is, we have too many of these colored codfish in some parts of the South, especially in the towns.

While I was in Macon, quite a spectacle was exhibited on the street, in the obsequies of one of our slave gentry. The deceased had been attached as a drummer to one of our volunteer companies, the band of which accompanied the body to the grave. The funeral cortège was truly striking. The body was borne through the principal streets in a handsome hearse, fringed with sable, and preceded by the band of the company, playing funeral marches, while, following after, came a long procession of negroes, in decent attire, and a portion riding in carriages. Yes! negroes actually riding in carriages, hired each at eight dollars a day! What, my dear C., will Mrs. Stowe and the nigger worshippers say now of all this "*fuss about a dead nigger?*"—a deprecation, you will recollect, of mass'r Legree!

Let them say what they please, say I, as long as they cannot get our negroes away from us, and kill them off in their own unfeeling land with cold, nakedness, and hunger. I am not ashamed, my dear C., to confess to be attached by affection to some of the faithful slaves of our family, to have sent them remembrances in absence, and, in my younger days, to have made little monuments over the grave of my poor "mammy." Do you think I could ever have borne to see her consigned to the demon abolitionist, man or woman, and her lean, starved corpse rudely laid in a pauper's grave? No! At this moment my eyes are tenderly filled with tears when I look back through the mists of long years upon the image of that dear old slave, and recollect how she loved me in her simple manner; how, when chided even by my mother, she would protect and humor me; and how, in the long days of summer, I have wept out my boyish passion on her grave. Yours truly, E. A. P.

To D. M. C., Esq., N. Y.

LETTER III.

BRIARCLIFF, VIRGINIA, 1858.

MY DEAR C——: I have been reflecting how illusory and fallacious are our poor human doctrines of happiness. What is happiness?—a question often proposed and often answered by enumerations of pleasures and gifts of fortune. But we cannot analyze happiness; we cannot name its elements; we cannot say what constitutes it; all that can be determined, is the fact whether or no we possess happiness, and that fact is one of individual consciousness. Happiness is a fact of consciousness: it is subjective; it is independent of all external conditions; and it is individual. The body may be surrounded by every comfort; the mind may be intoxicated by pleasures; the whole life may be illumined with fortune; no affliction may ever cast its cold shadow on the path; riches may dazzle; soft loves may breathe their incense; the conscience even may never accuse, and the wild pulse of pleasure may beat on and on; but the man of all this store and of all this fortune, when he explores his consciousness, may find the sentiment of unhappiness mysteriously and unalterably there. How wonderful is this!

Yet, dear C., there may be many who would accuse me of pressing a trite and very simple observation in thus speaking of the independence of happiness of all external conditions. I think this one of the great mysteries of life; and those who have *felt* its truth stealing into their hearts will think so too. Some days ago, I was walking in the fields; the sunset and the balmy air tranquillized me; I had nothing at that time to complain of, or to accuse myself of, and yet at that moment when I saw a poor man walking to his home along the cool shadow of the road, I suddenly, mysteriously, and earnestly wished that I was he, and might rest, rest from the weary world.

Yes, my beloved friend, God gives happiness to men, without reference to the circumstances that surround them; he gives it to the beggar as well as the lord; to the slave as well as the master. The doctrine of inequality in the distribution of happiness is impious and infidel, and should be rejected as a vile and corrupting dogma of the atheists and free-thinkers. The distribution is, in fact, where men do not pervert the designs of Providence, as nearly equal as it is possible to imagine; for even in the distribution of that portion of happiness derived from external condition, there is introduced a singular law of compensation, which adjusts our natural and original appreciation of the gifts of fortune, precisely in inverse proportion to what we have of them.

There was a time when I thought, too, how unequally happiness—Heaven's gift—was shared in by men. Often and acutely, when a tender and inexperienced boy, did I suffer from that thought. It diseased my sensibilities; it introduced into my life a dark and gloomy melancholy; it made me sorrowful, sometimes sullen, sometimes fierce. Well do I recall those feelings. In the midst of my own boyish enjoyments, when, having a pleasant ride in the old swinging carriage, or feasting on delicacies, I have suddenly thought of my poor little slave companions, how they had to work in the fields, how they were made to tote burdens under the summer's sun, what poor food they had, and with what raptures they would devour "the cake" with which I was pampering myself. Then would I become gloomy, embittered, and strangely anxious to inflict pain and privation on myself; and with vague enthusiasm would accuse the law that had made the lots of men so different. I was fast becoming the victim of the same fanaticism, the fruits of which we see developed in a senseless self-martyrdom, or in a fierce infidelity, or in modern socialism, or in the reckless spirit of "abolitionism;" or in any of the insane efforts to make all men equally free and equally happy.

But the bitter experiences of life have cured these feelings. In its sad and painful struggles has expired my juvenile and false philosophy, and I have awakened to the calm, serious, profound conviction, that every human lot has its sorrow and its agony, and that, as an Italian proverb beautifully signifies—"A skeleton misery is shut up in the closet of every heart." I am profoundly convinced that the negro-slave has naturally as much of happiness as I. What I disappreciate is to him an almost priceless source of enjoyment; the pain I derive from a thousand delicate griefs he never feels; all that I suffer from struggles, from disappointments, from agonies in a superior career, he is a happy stranger to. It is a very simple truth, my dear C., that happiness is *in the mind*—but when will the world learn the plain leson, wipe away the tears of all sentimental sympathy, and adopt, as the great rule of life, that every man should bear his own burdens; that the object of sympathy is individual; and that it is equally senseless and sinful to sorrow over lots inferior to our own, as to repine for and envy those which are superior.

I have no tears for the *lot* of the negro-slave; he can make it as happy as, and perhaps happier than, my own. I look into my own heart and write what I find there. Years ago, I left my home to adventure into the world, to seek my fortune tens of thousands of miles away; but my heart was swelling, defiant, joyous; I had glowing prospects, and was departing with a flush of exultation, which even the last tears that I dropped on my mother's bosom clouded but for a moment. But when I stood waiting for the boat along the little muddy canal, where began my journey, that was by progressive stages at last to enter upon the great ocean, and when poor old gray-headed Uncle Jim came down to the bank, tottering under my fine trunk, and stood watching my departure with loud, fervent blessings, my heart was struck with a peculiar grief. I thought that while I was going out to the world, to taste its innumerable joys, to see its fine sights, to revel in its fine linens, its wines, and its dissipations, here was poor, good old Uncle Jim to go back along the old wagon rut through the woods to his log cabin, to return to the drudgery of the stupid old fields, condemned never to see the fine world, never to taste its pleasures, never to feel the glow of its passionate joys, but to die like the clod, which alone was to mark his grave. So I thought when I left Uncle Jim on the canal bank, bewailing his "little young mass'r's" departure; (but considerately provided by me with two whole dollars to console him with a modicum of whiskey, molasses, and striped calicoes, at the grocery that stood hard by.)

Well, dear C., I went out into the world. I went first to California, and for four years there I think I learned some lessons that will last me through life. I had lost none of my buoyancy when I first stepped on old "Long Wharf," and took my first drink of genuine strychnine whiskey at an old shanty that stood curiously at the head of the wharf, surmounted by an immense wooden figure of "the Wandering Jew." I went boldly and buoyantly to work the moment I landed. Well, it is needless to repeat to you here the story of my trials, my successes, and my dread reverses. When the world treated me most roughly—when I writhed in all the agony of the defeat, self-distrust, and self-contempt of a sensitive ambition—when poverty-stricken I worked along one of the little streams that ran through a pine glade of the Sierra, and when I buried my only friend Mac there, high up on the hill-side, that the gold-diggers might never disturb his dust, and lay down at night in despair, waking up with the demoniac joys of a reckless life burning in my heart, burning out my life—friendless, moneyless, agonized—with such experiences of my own of the life of this world, I had very little sympathy left, I assure you, for buck negroes "pining in their chains," or any other sort of sentimental barbarians. I just felt that every man has his own burden to bear in this life; that, while (I hope to God) I would always be found ready to sympathize with and assist any individual tangible case of suffering, I would never be such a fool thereafter as to make the abstract lots of men in this world an object of sympathy. I venture to say that I have suffered more of unhappiness in a short worldly career than ever did my " Uncle Jim" or any other well conditioned negro slave in a whole lifetime. How many of us, who are blessed with so many external gifts of fortune, can lay our hands on aching, unsatisfied hearts, and say the same!

I am persuaded, my dear C., that the sympathy of the abolitionists with the negro slave is entirely sentimental in its source. They associate with the idea inspired by that terrible word ' slavery" the poetic and fiendish horrors of chains, scourges, and endless despair. They never pause to reflect how much better is the lot of the sable son of Ham, as a slave on a Southern plantation well cared for, and even religiously educated, than his condition in Africa, where he is at the mercy of both men and beasts, in danger of being eaten up bodily by his enemy, or being sacrificed to the Fetish or in the human hecatombs, by which all state occasions are said to be celebrated in the kingdom of Dahomey. Indeed, these foolish abolitionists, under a sentimental delusion, are brought to regard the condition of the negro in Africa as one of simple, poetic happiness, while associating with the idea of his " slavery" a thousand horrors of imagination. If you will hunt up a poem by James Montgomery, entitled " *The West Indies*," which was written during the early days of the British " abolitionists," and used as a most powerful appeal in their cause, being published with the most profuse and costly illustrations, you will find the same poetic and delusive pictures of the condition of the negro in Africa on the one hand, and his lot as a slave on the other, which exercise so great an influence on the weak imaginations of the present day. I copy some characteristic passages. Here is the picture of the negro at home:

"Beneath the beams of brighter skies,
His home amidst his father's country lies;
There with the partner of his soul he shares
Love-mingled pleasures, love-divided cares;
There, as with nature's warmest filial fire,
He soothes his blind and feeds his helpless sire,
His children, sporting round his hut, behold
How they shall cherish him when he is old.
Trained by example, from their tenderest youth,
To deeds of charity and words of truth.
Is he not blest? Behold, at close of day,
The negro village swarms abroad to play;
He treads the dance, through all its rapturous rounds
To the wild music of barbarian sounds."

But the negro, (according to our poet) is rudely snatched away from this poetic home of peace, loveliness, virtue, rapture, &c., &c., and is condemned to "*slavery*," condemned to endure

"The slow pangs of solitary care—
The *earth-devouring* anguish of despair;
When toiling, fainting, in the land of canes,
His spirit wanders to his native plains,
His little lovely dwelling there he sees,
Beneath the shade of his paternal trees—
The home of comfort."

Is not all this very absurd? But it is just such stuff on which are fed the weak, fanatical imaginations of our modern abolitionists and shriekers. Here, again, is a picture, by our poet, of a slave proprietor, which will suit to a nicety the modern New-England conception of a Southern "nigger-driver."

"See the dull Creole at his pompous board,
Attendant vassals cringing round their lord;
Satiate with food, his heavy eyelids close,
Voluptuous minions fan him to repose.
Prone on the noonday couch he lolls in vain,
Delirious slumbers rack his maudlin brain;
He starts in horror from bewildering dreams,
His blood-shot eye with fire and frenzy gleams.
He stalks abroad; through all his wonted rounds,
The negro trembles and the lash resounds;
And cries of anguish, shrilling through the air,
To distant fields his dread approach declare."

Now, my dear C., it is needless to say to you that we have no such ogres in the South, or to delay you with criticisms of these hyper-poetical and nonsensical pictures of slavery. I wish to recur to the more logical style, with which I started out in the commencement of this letter. I wish to say that the happiness of the Southern slave is not to be estimated by his paucity of fortune, or any such vulgar standard; but that we are to consider, as peculiar elements of happiness in his lot, his peaceful frame of mind, his great appreciation of the little of fortune he has (by a rule of inverse proportion), and his remission from all the ordinary cares of life. I will here add, too, in contradiction and in contempt of the poet's picture *supra* of the dreadful slave-owner, that a great and peculiar source of happiness to the Southern slave is the freedom of intercourse and attachment between himself and his master.

Instead of a slave-owner stalking around "with fire and frenzy," amid the "shrilling" cries of slaves, we will find the intercourse between the Southern planter and slave, even in the fields, to be generally of the most intimate and genial kind. Your own observation in the South, dear C., will doubtless attest this circumstance. You have seen, as well as I, a master kindly saluting his slaves in the field, and listening patiently to their little requests about new clothes, new shoes, &c. And you have, no doubt, also seen slaves, in their intercourse with the families of their masters, playing with the children, indulging their rude but singularly innocent humor with them, and joining their young masters in all sorts of recreation. It is these social privileges which constitute so large and so peculiar a source of enjoyment in the life of the slave, and which distinguish his lot so happily from that of the free laborer, who has nothing but a menial intercourse with his employer.

I might, dear C., give you a number of anecdotes from my own experience, of the intimacy which is frequently indulged between the Southern slave and the members of his master's family. I was trained in an affectionate respect for the old slaves on the plantation ; I was permitted to visit their cabins, and to carry them kind words and presents ; and often have I been soundly and unceremoniously whipped by the old black women for my annoyances. All my recreations were shared by slave companions. I have hunted and fished with Cuffy ; I have wrestled on the banks of the creek with him ; and with him as my trusty lieutenant, I have "filibustered" all over my old aunt's dominions from "Rucker's Run" to cousin "Bobity Bee's."

And then there was "brother Bromus," who had many a fight with Wilson and Cook Lewis, and who, besides being generally whipped, always paid the penalty for the fun of fighting by a sound thrashing at the hands of Pleasants, the colored carriage-driver, and the father of the aforesaid black youngsters. Would you believe it, poor Bromus stood in such terror of this black man, that even after he had gone to college, and used to spout Latin, and interlard his conversation to us boys with pompous allusions to college life, and with the perpetual phrase of "when I was at the U-ni-ver-si-ty," it was only necessary to threaten him with Pleasants' wrath, to subdue and frighten him into anything. But Pleasants was an amiable enough negro gentleman, and although he used Bromus pretty badly at times, he showed him a good deal of rough kindness, which B., to this day, gratefully acknowledges, and which Pleasants avers, with great pride in his manly master, was the "making of him."

Many a time, with my sable playmates as companions and conspirators in the deed, have I perpetrated revenge for such "rough kindness" on the old ill-natured blacks. What fun we used to have; and then there was no cruelty to mar the sport. We limited ourselves to simple practical jokes, and all sorts of harmless annoyances—would propel apples at Uncle Peyton when he got drunk in the orchard; and would send the negroes out of the fields upon all sorts of fools' errands, and lie in wait to witness their reception at the grand stone steps of the house by "ole mass'r," with his inevitable square-toed boots. No one enjoyed the sport more heartily than our sable companions, who, in all the affairs of fun and recreation, associated with us on terms of perfect equality.

But let me dismiss these desultory allusions to young days, to which my memory reverts with more of sadness than of laughter. I ask, seriously, who shall say that the black companions of our rambles and sports, who cheated us, quizzed us, fought us as freely as we did them, were not as happy as ourselves? Now we, their young masters, and they, have grown up to be men. From being companions in youth, they have grown up into slaves, we into masters. We two are pursuing journeys far apart across the fickle desert of life. But may it not be that they are still as happy as we? It is true that they have an humble and inglorious career before them, and must ever bear the painful thought of dying without leaving a mark behind them; but unlike many a poor white man, who has to tread the same career, not only without a hope of glory, but along the thorns of want and through great agony, they see manifested a constant care to provide for their support, to lead them along peaceful and thornless paths, and to sustain them even to the final close of life's journey to the grave. Is there no happiness in this? Is it possible that the negro, who has his human and rational wants supplied constantly and certainly, and who is indulged with so considerable a degree of social intercourse with his master, can be made, by the single abstract reflection that he lacks "liberty" (*abolition liberty*, mark you), more unhappy than his master, who may see nothing in his own career but a struggle with the great necessities of life, closing in a grave as readily forgotten as that of his slave? Who shall judge of other men's *happiness* in this world? Let the slave speak for himself; let the master speak for himself; and let the record be made when justice, the only equal thing—and that equalizes all things—shall be brought down from the heavens to be done upon earth.

Yours truly,

E. A. P.

To D. M. C., Esq., N. Y.

LETTER IV.

CHARLESTON, SOUTH CAROLINA, 1858.

MY DEAR C——: You will permit me to say that the expressions in your letter, of repugnance at the proposition to re-open the Slave trade, and of horror at what you esteem will be its consequences to the country, as well as to the abstract cause of morality, are, in my humble opinion, unjust to the facts of the case, and uncalled for.

In preceding letters, I think I promised you something about not discussing slavery as a political question in any respect. I believe that so far I have adhered generally to that engagement; and you will now indulge me for a moment, dear C., simply to say that there are many minds among us firmly convinced that the slave trade is almost the only possible measure, the last resource to arrest the decline of the South in the Union. They see that it would develop resources which have slept for the great want of labor; that it would increase the total area of cultivation in the South to six times what it now is; that it would create a demand for land, and raise its price, so as to compensate the planter for the depreciation of the slave; that it would admit the poor white man to the advantages of our social system; that it would give him dearer interests in the country he loves now only from simple patriotism; that it would strengthen the peculiar institution; that it would increase our representation in Congress; and that it would revive and engender public spirit in the South, suppressed and limited as it now is by the monopolies of land and labor.

But I recognize especially in the proposition to re-open the slave trade, the interests of the working classes and yeomanry of the South. The cause of the poor white population of the South cries to Heaven for justice. We see a people who are devoted to their country, who must be intrusted with the defence of the institution of slavery, if ever it be assailed by violence, who would die for the South and her institutions, who, in the defence of these objects of their patriotism, would give probably to the world the most splendid examples of courage, who would lay down their simple and hardy lives at the command of Southern authorities, and who would rally around the standard of Southern honor in the reddest crashes of the battle storm—we see, I say, such a people treated with the most ungrateful and insulting consideration by their country, debarred from its social system, deprived of all share in the benefits of the institution of slavery, condemned to poverty, and even forced to bear the airs of superiority in black and beastly slaves! Is not this a spectacle to fire the heart! As sure as God is judge of my own heart, it throbs with ceaseless sympathy for these poor, wronged, noble people; and if there is a cause in the world I would be proud to champion, it is theirs—so help me God! it is theirs.

But you doubtless ask, dear C., to be shown more clearly how their condition is to be reformed and elevated by the slave trade. Now I calculate, that with the re-opening of this trade, imported negroes might be sold in our Southern seaports at a profit, for one hundred dollars to one hundred and fifty dollars a head. The poor man might then hope to own a negro; the prices of labor would then be brought within his reach; he would be a small farmer (revolutionizing the character of agriculture in the South); he would at once step up to a respectable station in the social system of the South; and with this he would acquire a practical and dear interest in the general institution of slavery, that would constitute its best protection both at home and abroad. He would no longer be a miserable, nondescript cumberer of the soil, scratching the land here and there for a subsistence, living from hand to mouth, or trespassing along the borders of the possessions of the large proprietors. He would be a proprietor himself; and in the great work of developing the riches of the soil of the South, from which he had been heretofore excluded, vistas of enterprise and wealth would open to him that would enliven his heart and transform him into another man. He would no longer be the scorn and sport of "gentlemen of color," who parade their superiority, rub their well-stuffed black skins, and thank God that they are not as he.

And here, dear C., let me meet an objection which has been eloquently urged against the proposition to import into this country slaves from Africa. It is said that our slave population has attained a wonderful stage of civilization; that they have greatly progressed in refinement and knowledge, and that it would be a great pity to introduce among them, from the wilds of Africa, a barbarous element which would have the effect of throwing back our Southern negroes into a more uncivilized and abject condition.

What is pleaded here as an objection I adopt as an argument on my side of the question—that is, in favor of the African commerce. What we want especially in the South, is that the negro shall be brought down from those false steps which he has been allowed to take in civilization, and reduced to his proper condition as a slave. I have mentioned to you, dear C., what an outrage upon the feelings of poor white men, and what a nuisance generally, the *slave gentry* of the South is. It is time that all these gentlemen of color should be reduced to the uniform level of the slave; and doubtless they would soon disappear in the contact and admixture of the rude African stock.

Most seriously do I say, dear C., that numbers of the

negro slaves of the South display a refinement and an ease which do not suit their condition, and which contrast most repulsively with the hard necessities of many of the whites. I have often wished that the abolitionists, instead of hunting out among the swamps and in the raggedest parts of the South, some poor, exceptional victim to the brutality of a master, and parading such a case as an example of slavery, would occasionally show, as a picture of the institution, some of the slave gentry, who are to be found anywhere in the cities, towns, and on the large farms of the South, leading careless, lazy, and impudent lives, treating white freemen with superciliousness if they happen to be poor, and disporting themselves with airs of superiority or indifference before everybody who does not happen to be their particular master. Pictures drawn as equally from this large class of our slave population, as from the more abject, would, I am sure, soon convert some of your Northern notions of the institution of slavery.

I must admit to you that I have the most repulsive feelings toward negro gentlemen. When I see a slave above his condition, or hear him talk insultingly of even the lowest white man in the land, I am strongly tempted to knock him down. Whenever Mrs. Lively tells her very gentlemanly dining-room servant that he carries his head too high, I make it a point to agree with her; and whenever she threatens to have him "taken down a button-hole lower," I secretly wish that I had that somewhat mysteriously expressed task to perform myself. Of all things I cannot bear to see negro slaves affect superiority over the poor, needy, and unsophisticated whites, who form a terribly large proportion of the population of the South. My blood boils when I recall how often I have seen some poor "cracker," dressed in striped cotton, and going through the streets of some of our Southern towns, gazing at the shop windows with scared curiosity, made sport of by the sleek, dandified negroes who lounge on the streets, never unmindful, however, to touch their hats to the "gem'men" who are "stiff in their heels," (*i. e.* have money); or to the counter-hoppers and fast young gents with red vests and illimitable jewelry, for whom they pimp. And consider that this poor, uncouth fellow, thus laughed at, scorned and degraded in the estimate of the slave, is a freeman, beneath whose humble garb is a heart richer than gold—the heart of a mute hero, of one who wears the proud, though pauper, title of the patriot defender of the South.

I love the simple and unadulterated slave, with his geniality, his mirth, his swagger, and his nonsense; I love to look upon his countenance, shining with content and grease; I love to study his affectionate heart; I love to mark that peculiarity in him, which beneath all his buffoonery exhibits him as a creature of the tenderest sensibilities, mingling his joys and his sorrows with those of his master's home. It is of such slaves that I have endeavored, in the preceding letters, to draw some feeble pictures. But the "genteel" slave, who is inoculated with white notions, affects superiority, and exchanges his simple and humble ignorance for insolent airs, is altogether another creature, and my especial abomination.

I have no horror, dear C., of imported savage slaves from Africa. I have no doubt that they would prove tractable, and that we would find in them, or would soon develop, the same traits of courage, humor, and tenderness, which distinguish the character of the pure negro everywhere.

When I was last through the country here, I made the acquaintance of a very old "Guinea negro," Pompey by name, who had been imported at an early age from the African coast; and a livelier, better-dispositioned and happier old boy I have never met with. The only marks of African extraction which Pompey retained in his old age, were that he would talk Guinea "gibberish" when he got greatly excited, and that he used occasionally some curious spells and superstitious appliances, on account of which most of the negroes esteemed him a great "conjurer." Pompey is a very queer old fellow, and his appearance and wonderful stories inspire the young with awe. He looks like a little, withered old boy; and the long, fantastic naps of his wool give him a mysterious air. According to his story, he once travelled to Chili through a subterranean passage of thousands of miles. He also is occasionally bribed to exhibit to his young mass'rs, the impression of a ring around his body, apparently produced by the hug of a good strong rope, but which he solemnly avers was occasioned by his having stuck midway in a keyhole, when the evil witches were desperately attempting to draw him through that aperture.

Pompey had married a "genteel" slavewoman, a maid to an old lady of one of the first families of Carolina, and lived very unhappily with his fine mate, because she could not understand "black folks' ways." It appears that Pompey frequently had recourse to the black art to inspire his wife with more affection for him; and having in his hearing dropped the remark, jokingly, one day, that a good whipping made a mistress love her lord the more, I was surprised to hear Pompey speak up suddenly, and with solemn emphasis, "Mass'r Ed'rd, I bleve dar *is* sumthin' in dat. When de 'ooman get *ambitious*"—he means high-notioned and passionate—"de debble is sot up against you, and no use to honey dat chile; you jest got to beat him out, and he bound to come out 'fore the breath come out, anyhow." I am inclined to recommend Pompey's treatment for all "ambitious" negroes, male or female.

By way of parenthesis, I must tell you how Pompey's mistress scolds him. He is so much of a boy, that she has imperceptibly adopted a style of quizzing him and holding him up to ridicule, to which he is very sensitive. I will just note the following passage between the two: In the absence of the butler, Pompey is sometimes called to the solemn office of waiting on the table, at which elevation he is greatly pleased. Imagine the scene of a staid and orderly breakfast, attending on which is Pompey, having a waiter tucked with great precision under his arm, and presenting the appearance of a most complacent self consequence. Unluckily, however, making some arrangement in the pantry, he produces a nervous jostle of china. "Pompey, Pompey," cries his mistress, "what are you doing? Ah, Pompey, you are *playing with the little mice,* ain't you?" Pompey, in a fluster of mortification at this accusation, denies playing with "little mice." Ah, yes, Pompey, I know you want to have a little play—here, Martha, Sally, take Pompey out into the yard and let him play." The two maid-servants approach poor old uncle Pompey in a most serious manner, to take him out to play, but he shoves them aside, and crestfallen, and with bashful haste, retreats from the room; while the two women solemnly keep alongside of him, as if really intent upon the fulfilment of the orders of their mistress, to put the old fellow through a course of gambolling on the green.

Pompey is greatly cut up by such scoldings; and to be made a jest of before the genteeler and more precise servants, is his especial punishment and pain in this world.

I must confess for myself a strong participation in Pompey's contempt for "town niggers." Whenever he espies a sable aristocrat, he uses the strongest expression of disgust, "dam jumpy fish," etc.; and then he will discourse of how a good nigger should do his work soberly and faithfully, illustrating the lesson always by indicating what he does, while Henry, a more favored slave, has nothing, according to Pompey's account, to do, but to recline in an easy chair and eat "cake." I agree with Pompey, as to what constitutes a useful and respectable negro, and tell him that we shall soon have some such from the country from which he came, at which prospect he is greatly pleased. "Ah, Mass'r," says he, "dat is de nigger dat can do your work; he de chile dat can follow arter the beast, like dis here," tugging away and gee-hawing while he speaks, at the hard mouth of a stupid mule, with which he is plowing in the garden. "But I tells you what, Mass'r Ed'rd," continues Pompey, impressively, "no matter how de dam proud black folks hold der head up, and don't love de mule, and don't love de work, and don't love nothing but de ownselves, I tells you what, I ain't but nigger nohow; and I tells you, and I tells 'em all, *de nigger and de mule am de axle-tree of de world.*"

The truth is, my dear friend, we want more such slaves in the South as Pompey, who while they can speak such honest and brilliant sentiments, will also be as humble in their hearts and as faithful to their work as he, and who will sustain the car of progress over all obstacles in the path of Southern destiny.

Yours truly, E. A. P.

To D. M. C., Esq., New-York.

LETTER V.

CHARLESTON, SOUTH CAROLINA, 1858.

MY DEAR C——: In your rejoinder to my letter on the subject of the slave trade, which was touched upon but lightly and incidentally, you charge me with preaching "disunion doctrine," and say, that "I have overlooked the political consequences to this country of re-opening the African trade," and that "the first consideration should be, that this commerce could not be opened without risking the Union." I cannot, dear C., rest in silence under the charge of paying no regard in my recommendations for the legalization of the slave trade, to the peril in which it may place the permanency of the Union, especially when I am confident, if my memory does not greatly deceive me, of having suggested in my former letter (which you read cursorily, I suppose) that this commerce, by strengthening and satisfying the South, would confirm the bonds by which the two sections are united. I shall therefore vary somewhat from the original design of the correspondence, not indeed to go into a political discussion, but to call your attention to the relation which the proposition to re-open the slave trade, or the general proposition to strengthen and develop the South by new systems of labor, bears to the always interesting question of the perpetuation of "the glorious Union."

But in the first place, my dear friend, I must say that I do not agree with your judgment, that the slave trade cannot be re-opened by us except by infraction of our statute and treaty law. I contend, on the contrary, that the commerce in African labor can be carried on under the permission of existing laws. Observe that the African may be imported of his own will, as an apprentice, for any number of years; and when he arrives in the South, what is there to prevent him (although you say he cannot alienate his liberty) from accepting inducements to live in bondage? This I grant you, would be practically the re-opening of the African slave trade; but where exists the law that can suppress a trade which buys labor, not liberty, and which is really, in a legal point of view, conducted on the basis of enfranchisement. You may cry out that this is an *evasion* of the law; and I will simply answer, that you will find that it very often becomes necessary to evade the letter of the law in some of the greatest measures of social happiness and patriotism.

I sincerely believe, dear C., that with the slave trade movement, rests in a measure the great political problem of the day, viz.: the just elevation of the general condition of the South, as an integral part of the Federal Union.

It is evident that the great want of the South is a sufficiency of labor. Certainly no eqnal part of the globe can vie in sources of wealth with the belt of cotton territory in America, which, it is estimated, is capable of producing twenty millions of bales of the *snowy fleece* of modern commerce. Add to this the consideration, that within the borders of the South, owing to the singular advantages of a climate that partakes of an inter-tropical temperature, and enjoys in its change of seasons the peculiarities of the temperate zone, is a country capable of a greater variety of crop and agricultural product, than any other territory of equal size on the face of the globe. To develop this occult wealth; to introduce on the soil the many varieties of tropical vegetation of which it is capable—the olive, the camphor, and the cork tree; to bring into cultivation the thirty thousand square miles of cotton-producing land, which is now lying unproductive ; to multiply by almost infinite processes the product of our great staple, which now, under all disadvantages, is said to increase, according to an average calculation, three per cent., or about eighty thousand bales annually ; to expand our agriculture and infuse into it new spirit ; and to make the golden age of the most splendid fables of history our own, there are but wanting labor and the energy to employ and direct it. To attain this *desideratum* we have no other hope except the importation of labor from Africa.

The proposition to re-open the slave trade may be most truly characterized as a measure to strengthen and elevate the South in the Union ; and this being the condition of the perpetuation of the Union to us, as emphatically a *conservative* policy. In brief, dear C., *the slave trade proposition means Union and conservatism.*

The policy which I avow is, that the South shall secure to herself the utmost amount of prosperity and strengthen herself in the Union, which, as sure as the gentle hastenings-on of time, can only be preserved on this condition. This policy, then—the only one to save the Union—even if adopting extremest measures, is ever the truly " conservative " one.

I must confess to you, that I have the greatest contempt for that time-serving and shallow policy of many false politicians in our section, who decry a measure of Southern patriotism, in order to conserve our *party* interest in the North. I refer to the counsels of a certain class of politicians, who tell us that our party alliance at the North will be hazarded by free discussion at the South, and that it is to be cemented by our abandonment of the proposition to re-open the slave trade. Now, I truly honor our democratic allies in the North; but as a Southerner, I am not disposed (and I am sure, dear C., for one you would not demand of me) to sacrifice to their prejudices any measure of domestic policy which it is at once our right and our paramount duty to decide on for ourselves. Was the South to yield up Kansas "for the sake of the party?" Is this the beginning of the end? As God is my judge, I forswear, forever, this false policy in the South, to sacrifice any interest of hers to the consolidation or prestige of a party.

To the policy to strengthen a party, I would place in antithesis the policy to strengthen the South.

The South, my dear C., is approaching a critical stage in her political history, when she must act, if ever, for herself. The tendency to her enslavement, ruin, and dishonor, must be avoided by constitutional measures, or changes of domestic policy. The question is, how can the Union be preserved under the sanctities of the Constitution, and on terms of equal rights and equal advantages—how can the decline of the South be arrested—how can she be saved? She has now no means to develop her resources *pari passu* with the rapid progress, in this respect, of the North; she is unable, from want of labor, to expand her agriculture, or to follow where enterprise beckons; her public spirit wanes under her disabilities, and her constant sense of dependence on the markets and manufactures of the North; she is being constantly weakened by party identifications; her political prestige is gone; her peculiar institution has to bear a burden of censure, under which, even the best men of the South think it must sink, unless strengthened by new measures; the common territories of the Republic are being steadily closed to it; the black lines of free-soilism, in which it must languish and die, are being drawn around it, and the dregs of the poison cup are at our lips. In all plainness, what is to become of the South, if she is to remain in the Union without a change of policy? How is she to fulfil the necessities of progress and self-development, unless means to do so are provided by herself? How is she to be rescued from the fate which she has brought upon herself, and which now impends? The Democratic party cannot save her. The President cannot save her. She must save herself?

Will she do it? Let every patriot of the South answer for himself. Let him resolve that she shall not be argued into repose. Let him resolve that the inventions of policy to restore her strength, and at once raise and confirm her in the Union, shall not be hooted out by-party cries of "peace!" Let him resolve that she shall not rest in the supine embrace of party alliances. Let him resolve that she shall be called to the necessity of strengthening herself by independent measures of prosperity and power, within the terms, as such a policy must be, of honorable rivalry and of the Constitution.

Nor shall we, patriots of the South, despair of the result! Rather would we turn from the panic fears of disunion to the hopes of victory in new measures of Southern independence. For myself, I respect disunion only for its sincerity of motive; commended as it is, too, by many minds, and actuated as it may be by a generous spirit; but alas! one

> "Turned aside
> From its bright course by woes and wrongs and pride."

And yet, dear C., I regard disunion as unconsciously involving a moral cowardice, which puts to blush the courage of our land. Let the South, say I, stand or fall by the Constitution! True courage would dictate this course, even if the hope of ultimate victory, in the fact of the South's holding the balance of political power, did not commend it. The hard-fought field of constitutional contest should not be forsaken by the South for shelter beneath a divided flag; but the battle should be continued with the same weapons, while new exertions should be put forth to conquer by the power of the Constitution. We see, indeed, the necessity of following up each victory, and of devising new measures of Southern advantage and development; and to this necessity and its demand of a new policy, let us, ye true men of the South, God helping us, be true! But disunion is not a necessity. No! not a necessity as long as patriots still keep the field under the banner of the Constitution; and the prize of valor there is the victory of PEACE.

Yours truly, E. A. P.

To D. M. C. Esq., New York.

LETTER VI.

OAKRIDGE, VIRGINIA, 1858.

MY DEAR C——: The last lines I sent you from dear old Virginia, from the retirement of Briarcliff, were written in one of my fits of meditation, and I fear conveyed you but little of interest concerning my visit to the old familiar haunts of earlier days.

I have since been making a round of visits to "the kin," and I have been travelling most of the way on a canal-boat, at the rate of four miles an hour. Rather slow progress, surely; but I have not lacked for pastime. In the first place, I had to wait for "the packet," as the codgers call it, at a solitary "lock-house," where a bed could not be had for love or money, from night-fall until 3 o'clock next morning. But then

I had some charming companions in my vigils. A sweet, gentle lady, with her little boy, was there, and with agreeable and modest conversation beguiled the hours; and this lady, who kept her uncomplaining watch in the rude cabin, and who was dressed so plainly, and who even deigned to enter into the fun of a company of boisterous humbly-born girls, who also occupied the room, was, as I learned, the next morning, really one of the F. F. Vs, for she was met at the lock where she landed by her father, whom I at once recognized as one of the most distinguished politicians and gentlemen of the Old Dominion. She did not even forget to say farewell to the boisterous "Bet" and her tom-boy companions, who had so vexed the drowsy ear of the night before.

The boat-horn wailed out as the locks opened, and as I glided down the big, dirty ditch along the James, I turned for consolation to Bet, who in all the charms of rural beauty, was watching from the deck the scenery of the canal.

Bet was a rural curiosity, indeed—a pretty, coarse, and very ungrammatical girl, whose chief amusement the night before had been surreptitiously emptying gourds of water over the heads of her drowsy companions. Bet had been quite sociable with me through the night; but now that she was aboard the packet, she treated me with disdainful coolness. Approaching her, I hazarded the old hackneyed remark of canal travelling, that "I hoped Miss Bet was not suffering from sea-sickness." "No, she warn't sick a bit." A pause, and then I ventured to ask "if Miss Bet proceeded as far as Richmond." "No, it was too *furrer*.' The cause of her reticence and disdain was soon discovered. I found, to my discomfiture, that Bet had recognized an old beau in the steersman, whose city manners and glass and copper jewelry had quite extinguished me in her eyes. A dog-eared album told the story plainly. The following tribute I managed to transcribe literally, as with slow and jealous deliberation, I turned over the leaves of the record of Miss Bet's charms and conquests:

"When I from thee, dear maid, shall part,
Shall leave a sting in each other's hearts,
I to some grove shall make my moan,
Lie down, and die, as *some has done.*
(Signed) "PHIL. TOOLEY."

At last I reached my point of disembarkation, and I summarily dismiss Bet from my mind. I see again the beautiful mountains of the Blue Ridge in the distance, and the woods stretching far away across level plains to their base. How lovely it all looked, especially when with the whole scene were associated a thousand memories. In my childhood I had looked upon these distant peaks, and wondered about them. How much nearer and smaller they appeared now than when I saw them through the eyes of youth!—yet still beautiful, ever pointing through sunlight and through cloud to heaven, ever unchanging in their robes of blue, ever putting on at the same hours the purple and gilt of evening!

Having landed at W—— village, I prepare to pursue my journey on horseback. I disembark with an old gentleman, who, in the course of the voyage, had managed to convey to me the information that hewas a judge from Alabama, and had travelled a thousand miles on the "steam cars," and who had delighted the whole boat's crew and company with his learning and sententiousness, having advanced in a learned geological discussion in the cabin of the canal boat "that the vein of water was like the human vein," which illustration summarily closed all argument as to the distribution of subterranean waters. The old fellow was sound on the liquor question though, and proved himself "a judge" of good whiskey before retiring to his virtuous couch in the old "Rock Tavern." The sun was high when the black boy "Washington" roused me from my slumbers. Having bestowed "a quarter" on Washington, in abundant gratitude for which he wished to know "if mass'r didn't want his footses washed"—an ablution which the slaves of Virginia constantly perform for their masters with little noggins of warm water—I took up my journey along the old, red clayey road to the local habitation of my dear, respected old uncle. Here I spent a few days of delightful happiness, especially in company with my pretty cousin with the Roman name. But having found out that kissing cousins was no longer fashionable in Virginia, and that it excited my dear aunt's nerves, with one last lingering kiss of the sweet lips, I had my little leather Chinese trunk packed on the head of a diminutive darkey, and again embarked upon the James river and Kanawha canal.

After a round of visits to others of "the kin," I at last find myself the guest of that most excellent and beloved old lady, Miss R., and strolling about over the beautiful lawns and green affluent fields of Oakridge farm.

In the bright day, with the light and shade chasing each other over the fields where I wandered in youth, I recall many a laughing and many a sorrowing memory. I cannot write of all these. I must pursue the sketch of the slave, which is, indeed the prominent figure in the early associations of all home-bred sons of the South.

I find the old, familiar, black faces about the house. Uncle Jeames, the dining-room servant, is an old, decayed family negro, wearing a roundabout, and remarkable for an unctuous bald head, unadorned by hat or cap. Miss R., who has known him since he was a boy, still addresses him by the name of "Jimboo." Uncle Jimboo has a good deal of slave-pride, and is anxious to appear to visitors as one of great dignity and consequence in household affairs. He is especially proud of his position as general conservator of the order and security of the household, and any interruption of his stilted dignity is very painful to him. Devoted to his mistress, he assumes the office of her protector. Having in one of his winter patrols, according to his account, been chased by some forgotten number of "black bars," and having valiantly whipped "the king bar," and put the others to flight, it remains that he is afraid of nothing in the world "but a gun."

Peace to Uncle Jimboo! May his days never be shortened by the accidents of his valiant service! I can never expect to see the old man again; he is passing away; but, thanks to God, he, the slave, has not to go down to the grave in a gloomy old age, poverty-stricken and forgotten; he has a beloved mistress near by to provide for him in the evening of his life—a rare mistress, who, distinguished in her neighborhood for hospitality and munificence, has delighted also to adorn herself with simple and unblazoned charities to the humblest of all humanity—the poor, dependent, oft-forgotten slave.

And there is Tom, too, the hopeful son of Uncle Jimboo, a number one boy of about thirty, splendidly made, and of that remarkable type of comeliness and gentility in the negro—an honest, jet-black, with prominent and sharp-cut features. When I was a boy I esteemed Tom to be the best friend I had in the world. He was generally employed as a field hand, occasionally, however, at jobs about the yard, waited upon the table when there was "company," and on Sundays he rode in the capacity of footman on the little seat behind the old, high-swung, terrapin-backed carriage to church. I had a great boyish fondness for him, gave him coppers, stole biscuits for him from the table, bought him a primer and taught him to read.

There appears to have grown up a terrible rivalry for supremacy in the kitchen between Tom and his daddy. As time progresses, Uncle Jimboo becomes impressed with the prospect of being supplanted by his smart son, and, in consequence, he is very jealous and depreciatory of Tom. According to the former's account, Tom is a stupid boy, and is "good for nothing 'cept meat and bread." On the other hand, it is quite shocking to witness Tom's disrespect to his ancient daddy, whom he calls by no other name than "de nigger," and whom he artfully represents as "mighty shackling," and as making the last stage of life. The parental relation is completely ignored.

Here, too, lives Aunt Judy, who is associated with my earliest recollections of the days of boyhood. Especially do I remember the intensity of her religious sentiment, and how, for the faith of every assertion that any one ventured to dispute, she would appeal to the "judgment seat of G-o-d." Her hymns, her fairy tales, her traditions of old Sa-tan, her "shoutings" at meeting, her loud and ostentatious prayers among the alder bushes and briars of the brook—which latter used to be to us boys a great exhibition—are yet fresh in memory. How well do I remember the wonderful stories, with which she used to fill our youthful minds with awe, superstition, and an especial dread of being alone in dark rooms. We were told by her of every variety of ghosts, of witches that would enter through the key-hole and give us somnambulic rides through the thickets and bogs, and worse than all, of awful and terrible visions that had been afforded her of the country of the dead. She had a superstitious interpretation for everything in nature. In our childhood we were even induced by her to believe that the little bird which sang plaintively to our ears was the transmigrated soul of a little child that had been the victim of the cannibalism of its parents, and that it was perpetually singing the following touching words:

"My mammy kill me,
My daddy eat me,
All my brudders and sisters pick my bones,
And throw them under the marble stones."

Unfortunately, however, for the credit of Aunt Judy's Christianity, she was always very passionate, and our boyish plaguing of her was sometimes replied to in great bitterness. Dick, who was always ahead in plaguing, had no other name for the old woman, who was a great exhorter in colored congregations, but "the Preacher," or sometimes "Old Nat Turner." It was especially on religious subjects, which we found to be tender ones with Aunt Judy, that we thoughtlessly—but ah, how wrongly —delighted to tease and annoy her. Under pretence of delivering some message from head-quarters, Dick would call to her with an ordinary countenance, and have her come very near him, when he would bawl out, taking to his heels at the same instant, "I say, Preacher, what text are you going to preach from to-day." "Go 'way, boy," would scream out Aunt Judy, "I ain't gwine preach from nothing; if you want to hear preaching, go and hear your own color."

All the warning about the tragic fate of Nat Turner which Dick would give, Aunt Judy greatly despised, and would retaliate by asking that young moralist what, when he was "put an the lef' hand," which she assumed as a fixed fact, he was "gwine to say to black folks preacher den?"

From Aunt Judy's sentence of poor Dick it might be inferred that he was a bad boy. And so he was, after a fashion; and I fear that in this respect my humble self was only behind him in years.

When I was an eleven-year-old, "white-headed," irascible little boy, Dick, the elder brother, and myself were perpetually at fisticuffs, and the negroes would often egg us on to fight each other, which we would do in the most passionate manner. We used to have some downright terrible fights. Whenever we were captured by some vigilant house servant in the midst of hostilities, or were informed upon, we were made to smart under the rod, and what was more painful to the proud and angry spirit of each, we were made to kiss each other, while our beloved mother in vain spoke to us lessons of brotherly love. We hated each other thoroughly, I believe. How curious, indeed, are these boyish animosities between brothers, which in progressing manhood are so often converted into the most passionate loves!

How distinctly, how sadly, do I recollect one dark, cloudy morning in the years of our boyhood, when I ran away from home to escape well-deserved punishment for a fight I had had with Dick. Ah, how painfully do we revert to the memories of youth—the memories of our reckless wounding of the hearts that loved us best! My dear mother was at first not disquieted on account of my absence; she naturally thought that I had hid myself somewhere about the yard, and would soon return, sullen and slouching, as usual, to submit myself to the punishment I so well deserved. But as the morning wore away, and I came not, she became uneasy. Inquiry for me was set afoot among the negroes. Uncle Lewis, the cook, testified that "de last he see of mass'r Ed'rd, he was running straight down toward the crik." My poor mother was instantly thrown into the most violent and heart-rending anxiety. The creek, which was fed by a number of mountain streams, and often overflowed its banks, had risen, and was still rising from the recent rains; and it was certain that if I had attempted to cross the stream, which was not improbable, as I had often waded across its shallows at ordinary times, I would have been drowned in its swollen waters. The painful fears of my mother could not be quieted; they communicated themselves to those around her, and in an agony of tears she ordered instant search to be commenced for me along the creek and over all parts of the farm. Many of the negroes were mounted on horses to scour the fields, and the tutor and the whole school, including brother Dick, who trotted along in tears, joined in the search.

I was eventually discovered, but not until near nightfall, by Smith, the head slave, who carried me home on the back of the cart horse, "Old Windy Tom," in spite of my remonstrances and kicking. He was very short to all I had to say, which was little, as Windy Tom, who, for my particular punishment I believe, was kept in a high trot through the whole distance, jolted all argument out of me. I could only understand from Smith, that my mother was in a dangerous state from the excitement of her grief; that I ought to be "hooped all to pieces;" and whenever I remonstrated at his restraint of my liberty, the answer was that he warn't "fraid of my fuss," and that my "mar' knew what he was doing for her and hern."

Approaching the house I heard cries of anguish. My poor mother imagining me to be dead, was bewailing me with all the tears and agony of a devoted parent. Alas, how my conscience smote me! With my own cheeks wet with penitent tears, I presented myself to my dear mother, who covered me with embraces and kisses, and wept over me with happy forgiving tears.

Would to God I had been made to suffer pain equivalent to what I had inflicted upon the heart that loved me best in all this world! Going astray in maturer life, wandering away among its shadows, selfish, unreflecting, careless of that watchful and searching love which never forsakes, never forgets, and never ceases to watch and pray for the return of "the son that was lost," I have found the same easy, weeping forgiveness that took me into its arms the dreary night that I came home from the woods. I could offend and offend, ever in the hope of seeking that forgiveness at the last, and ever with the cheating comfort of amendment soon. One being on earth remained to fly to—one from whom to obtain forgiveness again and again as life wore on. Now—oh, my God, *now* I can only in tears look up to the skies, look to the beautiful, imaging clouds of heaven, and beseech the forgiveness of the angel-spirit that I see there resting and returning nevermore.

Yours truly,

E. A. P.

To D. M. C., Esq., N. Y.

LETTER VII.

BRIARCLIFF, VIRGINIA, 1858.

MY DEAR C——: In reflecting on the subject of negro slavery in this country, I have been greatly impressed by a characteristic, which, I think, has never been sufficiently recognized and dwelt upon; and which most honorably distinguishes it from other systems of slavery known to the world. Consider, dear C., that the American institution of slavery does not depress the African, but elevates him in the scale of social and religious being. It does not drag him down from the condition of free-citizenship and from membership in organized society to slavery; but it elevates him from the condition of a nomad, a heathen, a brute, to that of a civilized and comfortable creature, and gives to him the priceless treasure of a saving religion. Other institutions of slavery are found, generally speaking, to rest on systems of disenfranchisement and debasement. Look, for instance, at the Roman slavery. Its victims were obtained in war; they came generally from the ranks of enemies as civilized as the Romans themselves; or—more horrible still—they came from the ranks of their own free and co-equal citizens, who might be sold for terms of years by their parents in their non-age, or by their creditors for debt. Thus their institution of slavery was founded on the debasement of man; it was anti-progressive, depressing, barbarous. How free is the American institution of negro slavery of such ideas! *It rests on the solid basis of human improvement.* And in this respect, does its elevated spirit concur with the progress of civilization and of the religion of Christ, that, like the winds of Heaven, moves in its mysterious ways, gathers on its wings to and fro, and never is at rest.

Surely, God proceeds mysteriously to us in His works of love and redemption. While missionary efforts have proved, generally, so unavailing in the conversion of the heathen, we find great institutions and events in the common history of humanity used as instruments in the enlarging work of the redemption of man. We discover this in all that we know of human progress. The translation of African savages from their country as slaves--a great, improving and progressive work of human civilization—we also discover to be one of the largest works of Christianity, endowing a people with a knowledge of the Christian God, and they, in turn, enlightening us as to His Grace, and the solemn and precious mystery of the conversion of the soul to Christ. The work of gathering to Christ goes on, through all the tumults of the world, and notwithstanding its contempt of God's means and its own vainglory. Many developments in history, however unmerciful to our eyes, may be seen to be turned to the glory of God: and all our prosperity and progress is taxed for the completion of the work of the redemption of the world. On, on speeds and gathers the work in the changes of dynasties, in the founding of human institutions, in the intercommunications between nations, and in all the consummations of man's power on earth. Already it is said that the problems of the world—the political and social problems, and with them the great problem of Christ's religion, are to be aided to their solution by the swiftest and most sovereign agent that science has discovered in the world's domain—the electric current. Already may we declare glory to the Most High, and prophesy—oh, with what beautiful strangeness—that the lightnings, the home of which verse and the unwritten poetry of our natures have placed fast by the Throne of God, shall be sent on the missions of His love to all the nations of the earth.

But to return. I think the remarkable characteristic of our "*peculiar* institution," in improving the African race humanly, socially, and religiously, is alone sufficient to *justify* it. It would insult it to plead it in extenuation. Indeed, dear C., I venture to say that if nothing else was accomplished in taking the African from the gloom and tangles of his forests, and from savage suffering and savage despair, than bringing him to the unutterable riches of Christ, this alone should justify and even adorn our institution of slavery in the eyes of the Christian world.

We are accustomed, dear C., to hear of the paramount value of the religion of our Saviour—how far it exceeds all that this world can give or can take away. But we scarcely appreciate, in the practical intercourse of life, the comprehension and force of the truism. The best of us do not properly esteem it, in our comparative judgment of the condition and happiness of God's creatures. What, indeed, is the vainglory of the world, the names of free and great, compared to the riches of Christ and the ecstacy of a hope in Heaven, which the poorest, and, to our earthly eyes, the most suffering portion of humanity, may enjoy equally with—nay, in excess over—the elevated and sumptuous ones of the world.

You have read the story of Rienzi, the last and the most august of the Roman tribunes. He made a vow by the dying body of a young, sinless brother. In the death of those we love, there is a beautiful prompting of Providence to order our lives anew. We feel, in the depths of our nature—*and it is therefore true*—that the angel spirits of those who were beloved on earth and who worship in Heaven, still watch over us in tender sorrow at our worldliness, or in exceeding joy at our leaving the fleeting things of earth and coming home to them in Christ. But Rienzi, desolated by the death of his childish brother and the snapping of the last loved tie on earth, did not make the vow that nature prompted. He did not resolve to leave his proud manhood, to give up the vanities of his great learning, and to go back to childhood, searching in tears for the innocence he had lost there. He made a vow of bitterness —a vow to drown grief in enmity to man, in selfish studies, and in the pursuit of glory. And he succeeded in the accomplishment of his vow. He mounted the throne of the Cæsars; and all that treasure, luxury, or art, could yield was made to contribute to the pageantry and magnificence of his power. He was hailed by the extravagant populace as the deliverer of Rome and the arbiter of the world. Standing before the Roman people, he unsheathed his sword, brandished it to the three parts of the world, and thrice repeated the declaration, "And this, too, is mine!" He exhausted in this speech all the extravagance of self-glorification. But, alas! he could not do what the humblest Christian slave that waited on his pageant might do—point to heaven, and say, in the comprehension of all joy and glory, "But this, this is mine!"

Go, false servitors of Christ, ye who, on the ground

of religion itself, and in the garb of God's ministers, assail the institution of negro slavery, that has brought the knowledge of Christ to the heathen, and who recommend its excision by the sword of civil war, go and speak to the slave in our own country. Tell him he is assigned to an inferior lot, to life-long labor, in which he can never be great or rich, and can never taste of the applause of this world. And yet, how would you feel rebuked, if, pointing to heaven, he should declare, "But *this* is mine."

He has been plucked from the wilds of Africa, and saved to Christ. He is never an infidel, for he does not require, to establish his belief in the reality of the Saviour, expenditures of learning and processes of reasoning, and arguments about the prophecies and the miracles. He is not reasoned into religion (as no man ever truly was); but he teaches us, even us, an unlettered lesson of religion beyond all price—to cast down the pride of reason, and to listen to the voice of the intuitive divine spirit, telling us without argument, without learning, without price, of the eternal, irresistible truths of the religion of our Lord Jesus Christ.

Not for all your saintliness, ye red-nosed shepherds of God's people, who preach licentiousness and discord, and the contentions and parting of brethren, would I exchange the simple faith in the Saviour, of the poor, ignorant negro slave, whom you affect to pity. He has none of your learned assurance in matters of salvation; his ideas of religion may be fantastic, and may excite the laughter of your superior wisdom, that scorns the tender and beautiful ignorance that throws the charm of superstition around the lessons and emblems of religion; his notions of his state and calling here may never have been edified by your learned jargon about the Christian duty of socialism, of rebellion, and of the baptism of blood; but the great preacher Jesus Christ has spoken to him—not in lessons of discontent, not holding out freedom, or riches, or licenses, not addressing the lust of the flesh, or the lust of the eye, or the pride of life, but in precious consolations, in assurances sweeter than learning and research, ever found in their Bibles, and in lessons of perfect peace—the peace of the stricken, the weary, and the desolate, in the life everlasting.

It is true that the slaves' religion is greatly mixed up with superstitions, that it is ostentatious and loud, and that it has some comical aspects. But in his simple, earnest, affectionate, and believing heart, in his ecstasies of love for "Mass'r Jesus," and in his tenderness to whatever appeals to him in nature, are principles of religion as saving, I venture to say, as the precise creeds, and the solemn and exact manners of the churchmen. Many a death-scene have I witnessed among the slaves on the old plantations, and many a time have I seen those whose untutored and awkward religious professions amused me when a thoughtless youth, yet dying with the sustainment of that religion, joyfully, and with exclamations of triumph over the grave. No Christian philosopher, no preacher of politics or creeds, could add to that triumph and joy eternal, or could diminish the ecstasy of that inner assurance of Heaven by weighing the hopes of the poor slave's salvation in doubting scales.

Precious is the memory of the dead! And precious to me, my beloved friend, is the memory of the black loved ones who left me in the thoughtless, unremembering, laughing hours of boyhood, for that peaceful shore, where, now recollecting and sighing, I would give all of earth to meet them. Pressing upon me, and drawing the sweet tear from a nature that has long lain in the decaying embraces of the world, come the memories of youth.

I have often spoken to you of the old black patriarch, Uncle Nash, who led me by the hand to the preaching at the negro quarter every Sunday fortnight. This good old Christian man fell in harness, and died with on master but Jesus to relieve the last mysterious agonies of his death. He died out in the woods, where the angel had suddenly come to him. How vividly do I recall the excitement of the search for Uncle Nash, and the shock to my heart, of the discovery, in the bright morning, of the corpse lying among the thick undergrowth, and in the whortleberry bushes of the wood. But why lament the old slave, and wail at the terrible sight! The body in its coarse garments, dank with dew, lay there in the bushes, in the loathsomeness of death, but the immortal soul had been clothed for the service above, in its raiment of glory, and was singing the everlasting song in heaven.

He was buried in the grove, which my eye, from the point where I am writing, can catch on the warm hill, covered now with the blue blossoms of the thistle. Unusual marks of affection and respect were shown in his burial. The funeral services were read before all the negroes at the grave, and the younger members of our family attended as mourners; and, according to the negro custom, each one of us threw a handful of dirt on the coffin lid, as the last farewell. Many years have gone by since then, but I can never forget that scene of the deep, red grave, in which the old Christian slave was laid; and when the day expires, I revisit the spot and read on the white head-board that marks it, the words—"*The testimony of the Lord is sure, making wise the simple.*"

Yours truly, E. A. P.

To D. M. C Esq., New-York.

LETTER VIII.

ADDEBARRY, MARYLAND, 1858.

MY DEAR C.: I can recollect that once I entertained a belief, and found a dangerous comfort in the common doctrine that the physical pains of death were not terrible, and might generally be endured with ease. My present belief differs greatly from this deceitful impression. I now believe the pains of this dread change to be unutterable, and to surpass all else of the pains and sorrows of the flesh in exceeding sharpness. Reason, revelation, and the analogies of nature, all seem to me to point to this opinion.

Is it to be supposed, my dear C., that any change in nature so great and so vast as that of death—that the parting of so many subtile and close ties as those which unite body and soul—is accomplished without great travail and agony!

It may be that the failing body has not the power of demonstrating the last dread agony of the separation. That agony may be reserved until the body can no longer reveal its pain by demonstration or gesture, and thus be mercifully veiled, as it were, from the terror-stricken senses of poor, fearful humanity.

Have you, my dear C., ever witnessed, closely and steadily, a scene of natural death? In the quietest scene of this kind, there are yet, I think, terrors to those who exercise reflection and a just imagination upon its signs. How terrible is the cold, cold sweat, the heavy, dragging breath, the eye evidently—and it may be really—looking upon the veiled figures that stand by the parting soul, the gray mist that gathers upon its lids, and the restless arms reaching out and swinging in the dizziness of death. Oh, how fearful to have to pass through the unknown feelings of which these are signs, and to descend into the darkness of the last agonies of dissolution! How fearful, how awful to go down into the dark valley, and to meet there, in silence to all the world, the last, mysterious, veiled agony of death! Nothing can avert this meeting. We, dear friend, are to enter the valley, and alone there, with the world and friends and all shut out, to go down to death—to go down to meet, in secrecy with our God, the viewless, shrouded agony of the last. Oh, may that God sustain us in those moments! Surely naught else can. Then the comforter prays his last, and we have spoken, with the last effort, the last hard whisper the curious man extorts—then we leave behind all consolations of earth—then the world swims around us, and is gone—then our consoling friends fade from our sight and disappear—then voice and gesture to appeal for sympathy are gone too—then we are gone, gone away into the darkness and dumbness of advancing death—and then who is there to be with us to sustain the spirit in the last and real contest of dissolution that remains! Who but the precious Saviour, who in Heaven remembers the sufferings of Gethsemane and Calvary, and who has expressly promised to be with his beloved when called upon to tread the same path of nature's travail. Oh, how precious is this consolation! Here, here is the sweet lesson of death.

The impression, my dear C., made upon me by the first scene of death I ever witnessed, can never be erased or wholly overcome. It is the recollection of it that sometimes comes into the career of my life, and stuns the heart of joy, and has induced the thoughts I have just, in deepest sincerity, expressed of the terrors of the dissolution of the earthly tabernacle of the body.

It was the death of her who had held a place in my boyish heart, second only to the beautiful and lasting love we draw from community of blood—the death of a poor, old, black-skinned woman. The angel of terrors struck her in age, disease, and feebleness; and yet the scene of the parting of the spirit was one of the most mysterious and appalling struggles that ever yet appealed to my eyes.

Well do I recollect the night of gloom and storm, when the all-visiting messenger of death came in the darkness to the little log hut, and stood by the old straw couch, to demand the fleeting spirit of the old, worn slave. The family were awakened by a summons from the doctor, told in the usual, kind, suppressed manner that Aunt

Marie was dying. It was with a stunned feeling that I dressed and hurried out to the cabin. How I recall the solemn, relentless sound of the thunder which was rolling in the sky as I passed on to the scene of death! It sounded to me as the terrible voice of nature, saying, "There is no hope, for I am merciless; I am insensible, and must obey the forces that are in me, for I am nature." Never have I heard that voice but once again, and then it was amid the billows of a raging surf that swept over a wreck to which I was clinging, and then the sea seemed to say, "I am inexorable, I am obeying exact mathematical forces, and what care I for you." Alas! I felt not then that there was a God, to whose dominion and mercy man may look for his rescue from the boiling waves, from every scene of agony and danger, from every merciless law of nature, and even from the dark despair of a shipwrecked soul.

I approached and looked upon the rude bed with a beating heart, and yet with a strange curiosity. There, with eyes half closed, and with low, sobbing breath, lay the lean, worn body of the dying old slave. She was out of her senses; the soul was wandering forth in a dark and terrible delirium. Horror-struck, I gazed upon the scene of death, and yet curious, eager to note every sign of the awful change, stretching forward to see each token of agony and each print of death. For twelve hours I witnessed that scene, during which time the dying old slave was in the pains of dissolution, and never can I forget that long spell of utter heart-broken agony, mingled strangely with the most mysterious caprices of thought and fancy. Who, dear friend, can explain this curious psychology of the soul—these thoughts of utter levity and recollections of rude mirth, that intrude even while the broken spirit bewails its loved and lost by the couch of death, or in the last heart-rending but beautiful office of the burial.

Watching until the sun came out from the night and the storm upon the bright meridian of an autumn day, I saw Aunt Marie die. She died in a long delirium of pain, but not an unbroken one, as I believe. I watched it all—the writhing of those lips, the gaze of dumb terror in those eyes as they looked upon the hidden spectres and the weary reaching out of the arms above the head, that lay in the gathering cold damps of death. The doctor said her sane consciousness was utterly gone ; he consoled us with this, as we broke out into grief on seeing the agony of the sufferer—he said she probably felt no pain. But who can tell of this ? As the poor sufferer lay gasping and darkly struggling, but a few moments before the last, the minister came to the bedside and said, "Let us pray." Ah, what is she trying to do ? With what strange fancy are her hands reaching out and groping as if to find something ? The doctor at last divines the meaning of the gesture. He joins her hands together—this is what she wanted, to join her weak, trembling hands in prayer to God. An expression of peace lights up the face for a moment. Thank God, we say, that she is not dying in dark unconsciousness—thank God, that no mortal ever dies, as we may truly believe, in unbroken unconsciousness. The prayer is ended; all of earthly consolation is over, and the soul is committed to its God. A moment, and the lips are moving in a whisper. What is it? "Thanky, Mass'r Jesus," is caught from the expiring breath. And now she is with her great Master, and has gone. The doctor shuts down the eyelids; she is now in the dark last agony of which she cannot testify; death gives the silent, veiled stroke, and the body stretches out, sharp, rigid, dead.

This death scene, comforted by the man of God, and watched by white faces wet with tears, was that of a slave. But seldom is it, that the slave is left to meet his death as the white pauper in his rags and desolation. His master and mistress and the white family are always by to visit him in this great need of humanity. Indeed, when an old, loved slave (as Aunt Marie was), who has grown up with the family, the handmaiden of the old when they were young, and the mammy of the young before they have grown old in worldly care, is taken away by the equal hand of death, it evokes a sympathy and grief that many a white, saintly soul of your Northern Pharisees might envy, when he leaves the world unhonored and unwept.

There are angels in human form, and doubt it not, dear C., even among the slave-owners of the South. One I have seen, who to my youth was given, and who won my heart to love and worship her forever by her beautiful, angel ministrations at the couch where first I witnessed the appalling struggle of death. It was thee, my gentle Adelaide! It was thy calm and holy beauty, as, when all around were lost and idle in their grief, you sat chafing the cold hands of the poor, dying slave, with thy eyes ever raised in sweetest tears to heaven, and repeating the beautiful prayers of your faith for mercy for the departing soul.

Oh, mystery of the beauty of woman, how does the world misunderstand you! That world you court with bright eyes, and gay blandishments, and skilful dress, and painted cheeks. But more beautiful than a queen in all her lustre was the pale, gentle, brown-haired girl that attended the couch of the dying slave she had loved. There she sat, with no outburst of grief, pale, quiet, self-possessed, keenly alive to every imagined want of the dying sufferer, and anon turning her beautiful eyes, drowned in tears, to heaven, and repeating during the long, long hours the sweet hymns of the church. I had often admired some of these hymns; but an eloquence was therein I never before imagined when thou, my gentle Addie, with streaming eyes, and in trembling, sweet tones which told of the sinner's love of Jesus, pronounced the lines:

"Rock of Ages, cleft for me,
Let me hide myself in thee;
Let the water and the blood,
From thy side a healing flood,
Be of sin the double cure,
Save from wrath, and make me pure.

"Should my tears forever flow,
Should my zeal no languor know,
This for sin could not atone,
Thou must save, and thou alone;
In my hand no price I bring,
Simply to thy cross I cling.

"While I draw this fleeting breath,
When mine eyelids close in death,
When I rise to worlds unknown,
And behold thee on thy throne,
Rock of Ages, cleft for me,
Let me hide myself in thee."

And so Aunt Marie died—and numbered is she, the old negro, among those whom, with love-lit eyes, I can so often see beckoning to me from Heaven. How often, and oh, my friend, how plainly have I seen them standing on the edges of the white clouds of the day—and how often and how lovingly have I seen them floating on and among the still more beautiful clouds that are gathered from the day at the gates of evening! Yes, they are all there—the beloved parents, who folded their hands meekly in their age and died—the bright and noble brother that fell on the stained battle-field—the little sister that laid down her life among the flowers as a used toy—and with them and among them the dear, old, familiar blacks of my boy's home, their faces now shining with a radiance that has no distinguishing color of black or white—the radiance that is beyond the sun and moon and stars—the radiance of love to God and happiness in him. And there they are in sweet rest, and all in robes of white. Ever blessed are they in a love that knows no heartache, or parting, or reverse, or distractions, or degrees, but is even like unto the love of "Him who sitteth upon the Throne."

* * "Who to these can turn,
And weigh them, 'gainst a weeping world like this,
Nor feel his spirit burn
To grasp their so sweet bliss?"

Yours truly,

E. A. P.

To D. M. C., Esq., N. Y.

LETTER IX.

GREEN MOUNTAIN, VIRGINIA, 1858.

MY DEAR C.: It is clear that vain and unprejudiced minds are merely provoked by argument. How useless then, how worse than idle, to argue with abolitionists! In writing to you, dear friend, of negro life, I have purposely avoided contentious arguments about slavery. I have drawn some few hurried pictures of negro life and character, satisfied that the truth told of the Southern slave, in simple descriptions and anecdotes, will do more to cultivate wholesome sentiments on the subject of negro slavery, than wrangling sermons and essays. It is right, however, to state, that these pictures have been intended rather as amusements than as lessons.

In the course of the desultory sketches I have thus taken for your amusement, of the dark acquaintances I have made or renewed in my Southern sojourns, I have reserved for you some account of that most distinguished palavarer, romancer, diplomat, and ultimately a cobbler of old shoes—Junk. You will doubtless bring the hero to mind from the recollections preserved of him by one of your household, in whose early Virginia life Junk was a prominent figure. He was a short, puffy, copper-colored nigger, very greasy, always perspiring, and a little lame. "Missis Perline" can tell you of many sore experiences of Junk's shoe-leather; and particularly how, when by especial privilege, she was mounted on "hip-shot Jack" to go to church, Junk would waylay her in the woods at a distance from the house, and claim a lift behind her, where, by dint of his best boots and crutch, seconded by his young mistress' endeavors with the switch, the afflicted horse would be forced into all sorts of shuffling excuses for a gallop.

Junk had not always been a cobbler. To believe his own narrative, he had been a circus-rider, an alligator hunter, an attaché of a foreign legation, and a murderer,

5

stained with the blood of innumerable Frenchmen, with whom he had quarreled when on his European tour.

The fact was that Junk's master was actually once sent on a European mission, and proposed at first to take our sable hero in his company. Before leaving the limits of Virginia, however, he became alarmed at the risk of taking Junk among the abolitionists, and finally disposed of him by hiring him out as a shoemaker or cobbler, in a town at some distance from our dark hero's former residence. Junk never forgave his master for this unlokoed-for slight. It cut him hard and deep, for he was a nigger of "unbounded stomach." As an instance of the nice and becoming pride of our hero, it is well known that when Junk was in his working habiliments, he always professed to belong to the man who kept the shoe shop, and that it was only when he disported himself in his holiday attire, that he claimed to belong to the minister plenipotentiary.

But it was when Junk returned to the old plantation that his great importance began. He commenced by imposing on all the negroes round about, old and young, the story that he had actually been to France with his master, who still remained there, and that during the time he had been missed from the Green Mountain he had been lionizing in the famous city of Paris. The story took with the innocent darkies and gained Junk great fame. He became the oracle of the kitchen, and the negroes would crowd around him on every possible occasion, as he dispensed the eventful experiences of his pilgrimage. Some few of the men were skeptical, many were envious ; but Junk held his own, and was still the especial object of the admiration of the house-maids, who gave their sympathy and cheers in every combat he had with rival beaux as tributes to the truth of his information. "Twarnt no use," Miss Irene would remark, "to talk to niggers that never knowed nothin' bout de furrin country and de Parish, where ole mass'r was minister and out-preached dem all. Didn't Mr. Junk speak the langwig?—and dar is dat nigger, Colin, wid his swelled head, must always put in his mouth, and make Mr. Junk out a born liar."

Still Colin would continue skeptical. Junk, however, was more than his match, and had a ready answer for every question of the doubting.

The ideas concerning the French which Junk promulgated among the negroes were somewhat extraordinary. He represented them as a good-for-nothing set, much below the standard of nigger civilization, a sort of puny barbarians, who regarded an American darkey as a being of great majesty. Junk had slain Frenchmen, had treated the little, barbarous nigger-worshippers with disdain, and had received from them tokens of great distinction. To these points Colin's cross-examinations were mainly directed. He doubted Junk's prowess; he laughed incredulously at his deeds of blood; and he even went so far as to dispute the assertion of Junk's intimacy "wid barbarians dat were white folks," and to contend that his friend, the count, was some old "no count" nigger he had come across among the benighted regions outside of Ole Virginny.

We boys used often to join the crowd of Junk's listeners, and would have our own amusement in quizzing the old cobbler. "I suppose, Uncle Junk," Dick would say, "when you were in Paris you saw the Palais Royal."

"Saw de *Paris Lawyers*, young mass'r! Why, in course I did. You see when I got dere, I went to de courthouse to hear 'em plead. And when I come in, de Paris lawyers were pleading in French; but when dey seed me, dey den commence pleadin in Amerikin."

This compliment of the Paris Bar to Junk would be doubted by the skeptical Colin, who would again come up to the attack.

"I say, big hoss, I hope you didn't disgrace Ole Virginny by wearing dose boots in de city"—referring contemptuously to Junk's immense cowhide boots, which showed the deformity of one of his feet.

But Junk was always ready for the attack; and immediately remarked with a serious and gloomy look, that he had once killed a certain small Frenchman who had insulted his boots.

"How was it, Junk?"

"Well, you see I was walkin in de garden wid my breeches tucked down in my boots, when two of dese mean Frenchmen come along, and de one to toder cast an insult on my boots, cos you see he didn't know dat I knowd de langwig and could hear him. Well, I wouldn't stan no insult from no Frenchman, no how; so I jes struck him wid my nerves. And one lick was jes enuf—it killed de man; and dey sent for de secretary to sot on him."

"But what did he say about de boots, big hoss?" would inquire the persistent Colin.

"Well, you see de man talked French, and tain't while to tell dat to poor ignorant black trash like you."

But Colin was pressing. He wanted to hear Junk's French. The housemaids too, desired a specimen of the same, if Mr. Junk would kindly consent to put his rival down. "Dat nigger Colin had too much sass any-how—Mr. Junk, *won't* you please say what de French-man say?"

"Well," replied Junk, with a sudden jerk of conde-scension, "de man didn't say much. He say '*Poly glot sots*,' and de Amerikin for dat, you know, is 'de boots brought de fool.'"

And while all joined in laughing at Colin's discom-fiture, Junk would make his retreat good, walking off with a careless and provoking whistle.

Poor Junk! His travels were never more extended beyond the slopes of the Green Mountain. He was settled down as cobbler for the plantation; unable to revisit, except in fancy, the beautiful world he had traversed as diplomat, man-slayer and circus-rider—for Junk, according to his own account, had also been, in his various transmigrations, the star of a circus, and was accustomed to perform the feat of bearing five men around the ring "on his nerves."

The last I saw of the old cobbler in his decay, was when he was arraigned before a country magistrate, for having wounded with a scythe blade a negro on a neighboring plantation.

The sum of the evidence was that Junk had been surprised in his attentions to Nutty's wife, and in the scuffle that ensued had nearly chopped the jealous husband's arm off. A counter charge of assault and battery was also preferred against Nutty.

The miserable Nutty stood with his wound upon his arm exposed to view, raw and agape, as if to plead for him. He had no eloquent advocate to plead for the sanctities of his home. He had no wanton judge to listen to excuses of insanity. He had no committees of matrons to uphold him; no crawling serpent in the stolen livery of Heaven to tell him he had done right. He was a slave, and must submit to the law.

On the other hand, Junk was greatly at his ease,

losing neither his accustomed plausibility nor pompousness. Of course, being in the presence of his master, he was very insolent to the magistrate ; and he gave in his evidence with his accustomed falseness, and with an air that was by no means conciliatory of mercy, to the following effect :

" Name, Junk Jefferson. Dunno how ole I is—was boy 'long wid mass'r Tudor. Never was hooped before for nothin' ; never run arter other folk's wives—humph! —leave dat to de white folks" (magistrate looks indignant). " Nutty sassed me all for nothin'. Call me cuss words, and beat me. So when he come comvortin round me, I tell de nigger go way, I didn't want to hurt him, cos you see"—(with magnanimity)—" de chile was much younger dan I was. And den when he come gin me, and I had a piece of cradle blade in my hand dat I had jes found, he hit up he arm 'gainst it, and den he holler for de white folks—and den de dog come, and den 'twas ' Lord foot help body ;' and den you may know how dat was, Boss."

There was no other alternative for the magistrate but to sentence Junk to the lash. But it would not do, thought the wise man, to grant any great deal more to one litigant than another. So poor Nutty was also condemned to punishment. The sentence was, that Junk should have thirty-nine lashes, and Nutty, fifty ; those for Junk to be laid on by Nutty's overseer, and those for Nutty by Junk's overseer.

And so the matter was finally arranged to satisfy the punctilios of the masters, who attended the trial at the cross-road, somewhat in the character of opposite lawyers. The whippings were administered on the spot. The unhappy and discomfited Nutty took his with the touching sing-song of the negro under the lash; while Junk firmly restrained his voice, hustled on his shirt, and left the bowers of justice with a hateful gleam of triumph in his eyes.

...... "Equal and exact justice to all men!" Alas, the phrase is irony, not only on the slave plantations, but on how many other scenes constantly passing before us in the history of society and in the dioramas of the world.

Yours truly, E. A. P.

To D. M. C., Esq., New-York.

LETTER X.

WASHINGTON CITY, D. C., 1858.

MY DEAR C——: The remarks you have on more than one occasion addressed to me, to the effect that in both the natural and political course of events in this country, slavery was destined to disappear, have induced me to pay to this question considerable and especial reflection. And to my mind the question has assumed vast proportions. It has risen above the partisan questions of the day—risen above all local and passing excitements, presenting itself to me as a great problem, involving the largest interests of the world.

In this catholic view, I may treat the question of the extension of the negro slavery of the South. Not as a question between parties, or between sections, or between conflicting prejudices shall I regard it, but as an element to be solved in the mighty problem of who shall lead the world's progress, and who shall be the founders of its greatest empire of industry.

It is this question: shall the institution which has built up the commerce and industry of such large portions of the civilized world, that has so identified itself with the progress of the age, that is so beneficent to national strength and character, that secures the bulwarks of social conservatism, that inspires with independence, refines the soul, and nourishes a graceful pride; shall an institution at once so powerful and so polishing, be condemned to extinction, or shall it continue to flourish and gather strength and beneficence in the coming time?

True, I see with you, my friend, that slavery is losing *political* ground in this country, and that barriers are already erected to its extension in the West, (which is the present direction of our new settlements) that perhaps will never be surmounted. But I see other prospects.

Looking into the possibilities of the future, regarding the magnifient country of tropical America, which lies in the path of our destiny on this continent, we may see an empire as powerful and gorgeous as ever was pictured in our dreams of history. What is that empire? It is an empire founded on military ideas; representing the noble peculiarities of Southern civilization; including within its limits the isthmuses of America and the regenerated West Indies; having control of the two dominant staples of the world's commerce—cotton and sugar; possessing the highways of the world's commerce; surpassing all empires of the age in the strength of its geographical position; and, in short, combining elements of strength, prosperity, and glory, such as never before in the modern ages have been placed within the reach of a single government.

What a splendid vision of empire! How sublime in its associations! How noble and inspiriting the idea, that upon the strange theatre of tropical America, once, if we may believe the dimmer facts of history, crowned with magnificent empires and flashing cities and great temples, now covered with mute ruins, and trampled over by half-savages, the destiny of Southern civilization is to be consummated in a glory brighter even than that of old, the glory of an empire, controlling the commerce of the world, impregnable in its position, and representing in its internal structure the most harmonious of all the systems of modern civilization.

The magnificent ruins of Thebes,

> "The world's great Empress on the Egyptian plain,"

or the snow-white ruins of the ancient city of Palmyra, standing in the yellow sand of the desert, are well accounted to be sublime. But standing in the deep shade and hush of the tropical forests of America, are similar monuments of sublimity, around which, too, we can hear voices calling to us out of the gathered gloom of time. In the darkness and tangles of the forest, stand the ruins of immense cities and the splendid monuments of a strange religion. And it is to these magnificent fields of romance that the manifest destiny of the South invites us. It is to rebuild these ancient cities, to emulate this ancient magnificence, and to found anew the empire of tropical America, that our posterity may be called.

Ever since its first discovery, the Great American Isthmus, connecting the two large table lands of North and South America has attracted the regards of the world. It has particularly excited the jealous and grasping spirit of England. And it has been in the contest for the control of its transits, that she has founded an impostured dominion in Central America; has uniformly thwarted the progress of American interests in that quarter; and has, under the disguise of concessions, sought to prevail upon our government to renounce all dominion, at any time, in a country marked for our inheritance in the future.

Treacherously, has England struggled for the mastery in this country. Persistently has she wronged our government by the arts and anfractuous cunning of her diplomacy. But—believe it, dear friend—this cannot continue. The day approaches, when the American people will take this subject out of the hands of diplomacy. The signs of this approaching day are gathering. A glorious emblem is in the skies. It is that of the eagle and the serpent; the eagle stooping and snatching from the earth a glittering serpent, and, as the glorious bird sweeps onward and upward with his loud scream of exultation, he is seen to tear it in pieces with his talons, and the glittering scales are falling in the sunshine.

What is the "Monroe Doctrine"—the doctrine that the American continents are "not to be considered as subject for future colonization by any European powers?" What is this but the honored language of self-protecting and progressive American liberty?

The object, as well as intention, of the enforcement of the Monroe doctrine in Central America, would be but the legitimate one of a reversion of that country to its natural destiny. We are sworn, by a solemn declaration of policy, and by the eternal oath of American liberty, to protect the fulfilment of that destiny against foreign disturbance; and if the fact be that such destiny left free points to our advantage, it only fortifies a right, and recommends a duty by policy.

I do not, my dear C., speak of the political fate of Central America in the absurd sense, and with the supine satisfaction of the fatalist; but as a history of the future, capable of a degree of certainty, and resolving itself into a destiny which is morally manifest—one made manifest by a history of disorder and crime, and assured by the curse of fratricidal blood!

One step toward the accomplishment of this destiny; one advance toward the rearing of that great Southern Empire, whose seat is eventually to be in Central America, and whose boundaries are to enclose the Gulf of Mexico, was the memorable expedition of William Walker to Nicaragua, invited there by one of its revolutionary chiefs.

The objects of that expedition, my dear C., were for a long time extensively misunderstood. They are now being apprehended by the Northern people; they were long ago appreciated by the people of the South. It was to found in a glorious land of promise the institutions of the South, to extend them to other inviting countries of Spanish America, and, on the doubly secured foundation of these institutions, and of military ideas of government, to build up the great tropical empire of America.

This great idea, I have reason to believe, was conceived in its fulness by William Walker. Regardless of the clamors of the world, he pursued, in reserve, though with a burning spirit, the single object to which he devoted fortune, life, and honor. And while that world was regarding his expedition as a short-sighted and rapacious conquest, a mere raid, a vulgar seizure of a nation's territory, he, in secret, had undertaken one of the grandest schemes ever set a-foot in the Western world.

Crushed may be all the aspirations of one individual. But the idea of empire conceived by an unfortunate leader can never die from the hearts of the South. Ever perpetuated, and ever living, it will seek its accomplishment on and on, perseveringly, and at the last irresistibly. This, dear C., is a serious truth; and the American people, of all sections, of all countries, and of both continents, might as well accept the manifest destiny of a great, slave Southern empire in the tropics of the Western hemisphere.

We have the strange, prophetic words of Walker himself, when surrounded by his enemies, indicating the end, and prompting the Southern heart to its consummation. These words, dear C., I recite as those of a man, who, whatever the errors of his head, was yet a hero in his heart.

"In such a war as they are now waging against us, there can be but one result. They may destroy my whole force—a circumstance I deem almost or quite impossible; they may kill every American now in

Nicaragua ; but the seed is sown, and not all the forces of Spanish America can prevent the fruit from coming to maturity The more savage the nature of the war they wage against us, the more certain the result, the more terrible the consequences. I may not live to see the end, but I feel that my countrymen will not permit the result to be doubtful. I know that the honor and the interests of the great country, which, despite of the foreign service I am engaged in, I still love to call my own, are involved in the present struggle. That honor must be preserved inviolate, and those interests must be jealously maintained. Nothing but our own sense of the justice of the cause we are engaged in, and of its importance to the country of our birth, has enabled us to struggle on as far as we have done. We may perish in the work we have undertaken, and our cause may be for a time lost ; but if we fall, we feel it is in the path of honor. And what is life, or what is success, in comparison with the consciousness of having performed a duty, and of having co-operated, no matter how slightly, in the cause of improvement and progress!"

Beautiful, glorious words !

They are the words of Southern heroism—uttered by a hero, and uttered by him when the storm was beating darkest around the pathway he was then treading, and where his countrymen will seek his footsteps among the blood stains of the battle-field.

The explanations contained in the quotation I have made, dear C., confirm and enlighten the assertion, that filibusterism or rapacity was not the original spirit of the Walker expedition. It was not to be supposed that the Americans would shed their blood in a foreign cause for naught; they expected to acquire certain interests in Nicaragua, and a weight in the government; and they might have hoped that, in time, their civilization and industry, would win a peaceful and natural triumph over native imbecility, and change the destiny of the country. Such expectations and hopes were perfectly legitimate; but the result is hastening. The fickleness, the jealousy, the treachery, and the revolutionary spirit of the Central American people, that deny our countrymen the honors and rewards of a foreign service, and that would expel them from a country they have rescued from an internecine war, and baptized in their own blood, as saved for a higher destiny, can but tend to provoke and offer opportunities of just revenge to a spirit —call it filibustering if you will—not easily pacified, but active, invasive, persevering, and eventually to triumph, wherever it carries the Southern civilization and arms.

Turn we, for a moment, dear C., to the concluding portion of the thrilling language of soul-greatness that I have just quoted. How noble, heroic, and transcendental the sentiment that can hold life and personal success in such little estimation! How eloquent, indeed, of that high and ravishing enthusiasm, which impels, animates, and sustains, the noble and chivalrous leaders of progress everywhere—which is superior to success; which is nobly careless of human criticism; and which is its own reward, whether it leave its memorial of greatness in the splendid monuments of fortune, or in the nameless grave of self-devotion.

Truly yours,

E. A. P.

To D. M. C., Esq., New-York

LETTER XI.

GREEN MOUNTAIN, VA., 1858.

MY DEAR C.: You have repeatedly rallied me on the evidences of my sympathy with some of the superstitions of the negro. You tempt me, in addition to the particular subject of our correspondence, to devote a few pages to the great subject, in which white nature and black nature are both interested—that of superstition. I propose to do so by telling you

A CHRISTIAN GHOST STORY.

I am intensely superstitious. It is one of the sweetest consolations of my life to think that those who have perished from the earth may still stand about me—to think that they may watch over me in the darkened hour of contrition—to feel, when night gathers around me in the lonely chamber, that I can almost stretch forth my hand in the darkness to touch the features of the precious dead. The derisions of the world—the scoffing of the foolish-wise—the rebukes of the cold, dreary men of God, who measure the future state of the soul by rules, and brand with their contempt the tender and precious superstitions that God has given us, shall not cheat me of my consolation. There is a superstition above the vulgar standard of science. There is a superstition founded on the mystery of nature, transcendental, tender, and altogether lovely—looking from earth to the beautiful sky of heaven, its silver stars, and the long, long homes in our Father's house.

I do not know, my dear C., whether, in the desultory recitations of my boyish life among the loved ones of the South, I have ever told you of the bright little sister so loved by all the negroes, and so petted by the old, black ones, who claimed her as their darling mistress. She was the light and the joy of them all. She cheered the dark lot of the poor slaves, by exhibiting to them her own innocent happiness, by reading them the consolations of the Bible, by the ministrations of an angel Oh, there is no blasphemy in calling an angel of the earth her, whose youth and innocence, and gentle beauty came to brighten our dark home on the mountain like golden sunshine falling from a parted cloud.

But the angel on the earth had become an angel in heaven. Sweet Rosalie had died in her youth. Ah, how I remember the burial that so solemnly closed her forever from my human eyes! The gentle limbs of the precious dead were laid in the earth, when it was smiling with light and verdure, when the lambs were bleating in the meadow, and when Spring was hastening with its reviving kiss for nature, but its sweetest showers of tears in vain for the flower that had been plucked. It is needless to tell of the force of my affliction: that sorrow, at least is sacred. But year by year, my grief grew less and my love the more.

It was in the days of my mourning that I first began to take into my heart those tender superstitions, that make the negro's religion, to my consciousness, to my soul, a truer religion than that preached from the thousand pulpits of the land. The old negroes told me of apparitions of "their sweet chile," as they named my angel Rosalie, of seeing her in heaven, of meeting her spirit among the lonely trees at midnight. And I believed them all. I would steal away from the observation of the white family, to listen with passionate and thrilling interest to the stories of dear Aunt Matilda, who told me how my little sister appeared to her in visions of the night, with the angel-children of the Redeemer—and how they rode through the air singing songs—and how the spirit of her young mistress had told her, that the brightest place in heaven was not for little children, but for "the long-time mourner." And then she would chant some of her curious hymns. In what a fervent and beseeching manner she would sing some lines, which I cannot now clearly recollect, but the repeated prayer of which was:

"*Swing low chariot!* Pray just let me in!
For I don't want to stay behind.
Swing low chariot! Pray just let me in!
For I don't want to stay here no longer."

And there was another hymn of triumph and encouragement:

"Another little mourner strike Zion's hill!
And I heard from heaven to-day;
Rise, mass'r, climb the hill!
For I heard from heaven to-day."

Smile not, dear friend, at these rude chants of the poor negro. Examine them rather in your heart, and say if there is not nature's poetry in these untutored images; "the chariot" of the Redeemer's glory sweeping by, to which the poor slave looks with passionate longing—and then the "climbing of the hill," and the word of encouragement "heard from heaven!"

It is from the negro that I have learned my superstitions. It is the slave that has given me these precious consolations. It is he that has taught me and persuaded me that the spirits of those mourned as dead are with me still.

But to return to the story which I started to tell: One day Aunt Matilda told me, as was not unusual, that she had a message for me from my angel-sister. It was a curious message, unlike former ones of love and encouragement. The old woman delivered it with an ominous look, refusing to explain by a single word its meaning, which was hidden to my boyish sense, and yet awful in its impression. It was, that "*she was coming for me.*" Coming for me! What did it mean? Should I indeed see again my precious little sister, as the old slave had described her, with her golden locks clothing her in glittering beauty, and with "silver slippers on her feet!" For a long time my imagination dwelt upon the promise.

And now, dear friend, believe me—oh, do not mock me, but believe me—when I tell you solemnly, and speaking from all the heart can feel of truth, that the promise has been kept!

Many, many years after the message had been given me by Aunt Matilda, when I had grown up to manhood, and entered upon its serious years, I was taken down by a memorable sickness. It was a long, weary sickness, to which my memory reverts with a shudder. I had lain for many weeks in a slow fever, and was reduced to a very critical state of weakness. Everything was kept still and solemn about my room.

One night, I was lying in restless, broken reveries. The lights, which had been withdrawn by my nurse into an adjoining room, left mine in an indistinct gloom, a darkness filled with shadows. I was in an uncertain state, neither asleep nor awake ; but in an indescribable sort of stupor. Suddenly, I felt myself curiously failing. I can describe my sensation only as that of a sinking, like the running down of mechanism ; my mind falling away into a sort of lightness, then with unutterable terror grasping at consciousness, and then falling away deeper and deeper into the vagueness. I felt that I was dying. But I had no strength to call out. Further and further, I felt falling away, still grasping, clutching at consciousness, oh! with what inconceivable agony. One terrible effort—one more wrestle of agony, and I felt a sudden, boundless freedom, a sense of an unutterable expanse around me—an *aërialness* that human words cannot express. I was still in my chamber, but I seemed to touch nothing ; I felt an irrepressible lightness, and yet I was so keenly conscious, that I could hear sounds that seemed to be far away over the hills, and floating up to the skies.

A slight rustle by my side attracted me. I turned my eyes. Merciful God! it was my angel, Rosalie, who stood there. Father in Heaven, it was thy messenger. There she stood in the darkened room, with a countenance as white and calm as death, no earthly beauty there, no smiles, but white, white, and yet a thousand times beautiful in the deep, passionless, Heaven-sealed peace of God's beloved. I could not speak to my darling. An awful restraint was upon me; and when she beckoned to me, I followed, as if on air. All things seemed dissolving from me; the earth appeared to be falling away into shadows. I felt as if encompassed by darkness, and treading through it to an illimitable Beyond.

Oh, the darkness is breaking at last! The angel form before me, never turning as I have followed, is now growing brighter and more glorious. I see the great white radiance, to which her path leads up through the darkness. Oh, Gracious Father, is this the home of thy beloved! I see dimly as through a glass. But amid myriads of figures peopling this everlasting light, where no shadow ever falls, and no storms, no rent banners in the sky, or wars, or "garments rolled in blood," are ever known—amid them all, I distinguish white figures advancing to meet me Who comes on in the the bright raiment of glory so swiftly and happily? Who is she with the everlasting seal of peace upon her brow that comes to meet me? Saviour, sweet Saviour, will you grant me this reunion also!—for it is *my mother* that comes, it is my mother, reaching out her hands to the son that was lost!

I am standing on the confines of darkness, with one

step from it into unutterable happiness. My darling, my angel, Rosalie, turns to me. A smile of Heaven now lights up her face; a scarce repressed song seems to tremble on her lips. She stretches her tiny hand toward me. I seek to grasp it. But as I touch it, she starts, the whole scene rocks and falls before me into nothingness; and I hear the voice of Rosalie sweetly, sadly, saying, "*Alas, I thought you were dead!*"

Was it a dream you ask—a nightmare broken and changing into a dreamer's ecstacy. Call it what you will, let the world use the cold sneering term of "a dream" to conceal its ignorance of the mysterious communings of the soul, let it congratulate itself upon the easy explanations of the wonders of Him, who worketh visions of the night. But the day comes, when the "dream" of life itself shall pass away, and we shall stand, as I solemnly believe, in the reality of what was revealed to us in the night, and in the darkened hours of our lives on earth.

No, my Rosalie, not dead yet; not ready yet to cross into the light everlasting! But struggling on, considering all things of this world lightly, bearing its insults and its goads, putting away its quarrels, looking up ever to the better day, suffering, worn and weary, I pray to my Saviour, that a broken family may be reunited at his Throne, and that there, as on earth, my beloved and I may praise him together. Yours truly, E. A. P.

To D. M. C., Esq., New-York.

www.ingramcontent.com/pod-product-compliance
Lightning Source LLC
LaVergne TN
LVHW021423110826
845150LV00007B/2052

* 9 7 8 1 4 2 5 5 0 8 0 6 7 *